THE
OUTPOST
OF THE
LOST

Explorers Club Classics also available:

The Worst Journey in the World by Apsley Cherry-Gerard

A Journey for the Ages by Matthew B. Henson

Famous First Flights by Lowell Thomas and Lowell Thomas, Jr.

With Lawrence in Arabia by Lowell Thomas

The Shipwreck of the Whaleship Essex by Owen Chase

Thirty Years in the Arctic Regions by Sir John Franklin

North Pole Legacy by S. Allen Counter

THE OUTPOST OF THE LOST

An Arctic Adventure

By David L. Brainard

FOREWORD BY GEOFFREY E. CLARK

Skyhorse Publishing

ACKNOWLEDGMENTS

The Outpost of the Lost by David L. Brainard holds a prominent place in the literature of Arctic Polar exploration. The Explorers Club is proud to publish our edition of this book in collaboration with Jay Cassell, Editorial Director at Skyhorse Publishing. Adolphus Greeley, who led the Lady Franklin Bay Expedition, and author David L. Brainard were distinguished members of The Explorers Club. They both survived the harsh and tragic events that unfolded.

A special thanks goes to Explorers Club President Ted Janulis for his enthusiasm and support for this addition to our Classics Series. Geoffrey E. Clark graciously wrote a new introduction for this edition and contributed additional material. Thanks also go to Executive Director, Will Roseman; Curator of Collections, Lacey Flint; George Gowen; and Veronica Alvarado.

Jay Cassell understands and honors The Explorers Club's commitment to keep in print books representing excellence and challenge in exploration.

—Lindley Kirksey Young, The Explorers Club

Spring 2018

FOREWORD BY GEOFFREY E. CLARK

IN THE summer of 1876, an eighteen-year-old youth from a tiny town in upstate New York left home to attend the Centennial Exhibition in Philadelphia. According to his family history,

> He had a fine time viewing the wonders that heralded the arrival of the Machine Age and came away marveling how much the inventions had improved the world for people to work and live in. At New York City he had to change cars. He reached in his pocket for money to buy a ticket; there was no money. Too proud to write home for funds, the bankrupt sightseer took a ride on the free ferry to that ran to the United States Army Post on Governor's Island and joined the Regular Army. Changing into a uniform, he found a ten-dollar bill [worth $250 in today's dollars] hidden away in the pocket of his civilian shirt. But he was in the army now—Private David L. Brainard.

Whether by a stroke of misfortune or an impulse to venture beyond his rural home, his enlistment lead to his participation as a hero in what is arguably the most important (and most tragic) episode in the history of American polar exploration: The Lady Franklin Bay Expedition of 1881-84, colloquially known as The Greely Expedition.

Private Brainard was posted to the far west where he participated in the so-called "Indian Wars," rising over a span of only three years to the rank of sergeant. He saw action in several fights and late in life was awarded one of only two Purple Heart medals for wounds suffered in the Indian campaigns. If his motivation for joining the army was adventure and travel, the Wild West was apparently insufficiently challenging. In 1879, he volunteered to serve as a member of an arctic expedition to establish a "Polar Colony" only 450 miles from the North Pole, in what is now the northern-most part of Canada.

This ambitious and perilous project was the brainchild of a Captain Howgate of the US Army Signal Corps. It can be seen as an expression of the expansionist impulse that arose in the United States after the Civil War and the closing of the American frontier. Howgate promoted the enterprise as a US Army project. Federal funding was withdrawn at the last moment when government surveyors found his chosen ship, the Gulnare, unfit for service, but Howgate sent the ship north with private support. Presumably Brainard was already detailed for service on the voyage and departed as the only member of the military on board. On arrival in Greenland after a rough passage, the findings of the survey- ors proved correct. Following the better part of the summer spent repairing serious damage, the Gulnare returned to the United States. Meanwhile, Brainard obtained critical expe- rience in dealing with the arctic climate and its inhabitants.

Howgate was undeterred in pushing for his colony and by 1880 had found an additional, more serious rationale for government funding. An Austrian scientist and arctic explorer, Carl Weyprecht had convened an internation- al congress in 1877 to discuss the problem of finding out what conditions prevailed in the high polar regions, which had heretofore defied all attempts at direct exploration. The congress organized an ingenious scheme involving the cooperation of fourteen nations to establish stations as far north as possible, and there to collect an enormous amount of data using a detailed protocol that required the collection of many meteorological and physical measurements every four hours around the clock for at least a year. These large databases were then to be correlated to deduce conditions at the North Pole—a massive undertaking in the pre-com- puter era. American scientists lent their support to this

International Polar Year, and in the end the federal government committed to establishing two research stations, one at Barrow, Alaska and the other, by far the farthest north, at the site proposed by Howgate. This was at Discovery Harbor in Lady Franklin Bay, where a British expedition had wintered over in 1875-76 and had established the record for "The Furthest North," an honor held by Great Britain for over three hundred years. Thus the expedition had two objectives. The public objective was to undertake a serious enterprise to obtain data in cooperation with the international scientific community. Just as important but never officially stated was the goal of extending the reach of American exploration and wresting the record for "The Furthest North" from the British.

American participation was put under the command of the US Army Signal Corps, which at that time was responsible for running the US Weather Bureau. A civil war veteran and Signal Corps officer, First Lieutenant Adolphus W. Greely was put in command of the expedition to Lady Franklin Bay. When it came to putting together a party of military men and civilian scientists, David Brainard was an obvious choice, because of his demonstrated leadership abilities and the fact that he had previously volunteered for arctic service. Out of the twenty-four men chosen, Brainard was the only soldier with any arctic experience, the two others being Dr. Octave Pavy and photographer George Rice, who had also gone north to Greenland on the Gulnare in 1880. Greely chose Brainard to be first sergeant, meaning that he was the senior non-commissioned officer in command of the enlisted men.

The route to Discovery Harbor required the navigation of relatively narrow Kennedy Channel and Davis Basin between Ellesmere Island and Greenland. These are choked with ice except for a variable length of time in the summer, and sometimes not even then. The plan called for the use of a chartered steamer, the *Proteus*, with an experienced ice pilot, to transport the party of twenty-four men, a prefabricated double-walled house, scientific equipment and supplies for three years. In the summer of the following year a supply ship was to visit the station with mail and more supplies, and to return with any ill or disaffected personnel. Should the ship find the passage blocked, it was to leave its supplies on the Ellesmere coast at its point of farthest progress or at least at Cape Sabine on Pim Island in Smith Sound, 250 miles south. This was the location that ships could count on reaching every year.

In the second summer, a ship was to return to pick up the party, its equipment and records for return to the United States. In the event that the passage was impassible the second year the fallback plan was for the ship to return to Cape Sabine and leave a cache of supplies sufficient for the party to winter over. If possible, the ship was to await the party, which was instructed to retreat by open boats along the coast. If the ship could not remain, the party would winter over at Cape Sabine until recovered the following spring. Every detail of the plan had to be set in place before the expedition commenced, as there was absolutely no way of communicating with the party once it had been left at the station.

Even in retrospect the plans anticipated every contingency save one: the utter incompetency of the US Army Signal Corps in carrying out the relief and recovery operations. The first supply ship in the summer of 1882 was under the supervision of a private, whose only qualification was that he was the personal secretary of the Signal Corps Commander. It was unable to proceed more than a third of the way up the passage despite a month of maneuvering, but, for reasons that remain unclear, returned to the United States without leave any of its supplies as directed.

The recovery mission the following year was even more disastrous. The *Proteus* was sent again, but under the command of an impetuous cavalry officer, Lieutenant Garlington. And arrived at the entrance to Smith Sound early in the season. Rather than leave a cache of supplies at Cape Sabine and waiting for the ice to open, Garlington demanded that the skipper proceed into the pack. Within an hour the ship was "nipped," crushed, and sank. Garlington was forced to retreat in the lifeboats, leaving only rations for two weeks at Cape Sabine, with a note explaining what had happened. Of course Greely and his men at Fort Conger knew none of this. So when no recovery ship appeared, after two years of meticulous scientific work and setting the record for "The Furthest North" without loss of life or serious injury, the party retreated south according to plan—into a deadly trap.

This needs to be kept in mind while reading Brainard's contemporaneous account. Every member of the party was required to keep a diary to be part of the official record, and which was to be surrendered to Greely after the two years at Fort Conger. Thus this account consists of two parts: Brainard's official diary dates from his embarkation on July 7, 1881 until August 8, 1883. Whether he, like some others, kept a separate private diary is unknown. But probably everyone was circumspect in his observations and criticisms, knowing that what they wrote would become public. Brainard's diary from August 9, 1883 through June 21, 1884 was undoubtedly private, written in pencil in a small pocket notebook. But even here Brainard omits key events, some which are only reported in later annotations, if at all.

Certainly the personality conflicts that plagued the expedition are underreported. Greely was a self-educated Yankee from Newburyport, Massachusetts, who joined the army as a private in the Civil War at seventeen and received a battlefield commission. While not a martinet, he was serious and conscientious to a fault as well as perhaps a bit stubborn. His second-in-command, while well recommended, had recently lost his second wife to sudden illness leaving him with several young children, so that he embarked in a state of profound depression. When the two had a falling out over what was a relatively minor matter, Kislingbury resigned his commission but failed to get on the Proteus in time to return home, leaving him marooned without any official status. Both men were too proud and/or too stubborn to make amends, resulting in continuing antagonism, which in turn was aggravated by the hostility of the physician Dr. Octave Pavy. Pavy was a highly cultured, Paris educated "bohemian" with no respect for the military life. He had gone to Greenland with the Howgate Expedition, stayed for the year until the expedition was resurrected and in the process learned the Inuit (Eskimo) language and customs. He considered himself, with some justification, superior to Greely in arctic lore.

The conflicts between these three poisoned the atmosphere of the party, particularly in the winters when the men were confined to the station most of the time. But matters came to a head in a mutiny proposed by Pavy and Kislingbury shortly after their departure from Conger, an incident that Brainard omitted from even his private diary until its publication. The two proposed that Pavy, as party physician, pronounce Greely unfit, replace him with Kislingbury as commander, and that they return to the safety of Fort Conger. Given the disaster that awaited them this may have been a good idea, but it was in direct disobedience to Greely's orders. It was Brainard, who despite misgivings was loyal to Greely and military discipline, who quashed the incipient insurrection. Yet he chose not to record the matter contemporaneously. These antagonisms persisted until the last tragic days when all but Greely died.

One issue never mentioned or alluded to by Brainard in

the diaries or elsewhere is the cannibalism that undoubtedly occurred. This was clearly documented from the examination of the remains of those who had died, but was totally denied by all six survivors. Surely at least one must have known or participated. Could it have happened but been hidden from Brainard or Greely?

Even though it was widely reported in the newspapers shortly after the survivors returned, it was apparently too much of a taboo to merit discussion well into the twentieth century when only Brainard remained alive. It remains an enduring mystery.

Finally, Brainard is so modest in his account that we must read between the lines to realize that, without his leadership, determination and ingenuity no one would have survived. As First Sergeant he maintained discipline and morale when Greely was failing and the other officers had died. He maintained rigorous control of the meager remaining rations, issued them with strict impartiality and when a member of the party was found guilty of repeatedly stealing food, took charge of his execution. Perhaps most important, he discovered and devised a means of catching a tiny shrimp-like creature that was the only consistently reliable source of food. Virtually every day he would spend hours at the shore fishing with an improvised net and baits, bringing back up to thirty pounds a day—a total of well over a ton! Considering that they were only hours from death when rescue arrived, clearly Sergeant David Brainard was the hero who ensured that six came back.

When it came time for publication, Brainard's account was broken into two parts. The first half, entitled *The Outpost of the Lost,* is recounted here, and details the expedition from August 1883 through June 1884.

SALUTATION

Washington, D. C. November 1, 1928.

MY DEAR BRAINARD,—sole survivor of my Arctic comrades:

Fresh from Indian wars and scarcely healed wounds on the frontier, you volunteered half a century since for service with me in the Arctic Zone.

In the three years therein, with the lamented Lockwood, you placed your name high on the immortal scroll of fame by winning for our great Nation the honors of the Highest North, which England's distinguished explorers had held unbroken for three centuries.

In that Arctic service together we shared the perils of the drifting polar pack, the indescribable sufferings of an Arctic winter, without necessary clothing, heat, shelter or sustaining food. Together with our comrades we faced for nine months the prospect of death day by day, and were harassed by the sight of our associates perishing by starvation, or from vicissitudes in the polar field.

Your service in later years has been with distinction at home and abroad, marked by the same manly virtues earlier displayed by you in the Arctic.

Modern inventions spare the explorer of to-day from the dog and sled, lessen many dangers of disaster, and from the grim solitude that overwhelms man isolated from his kind for years,—as we have known it. This gives value to your diary, written mostly under direst distress. Thereby the world of the twentieth century may learn in part the extreme difficulties and deprivations under which explorations were made in the nineteenth century.

Your former commander sends this greeting a faint tribute to your merits.

A. W. GREELY

Major General, U.S.A., Retired; Formerly 1st Lieutenant, commanding International Arctic Expedition.

General David L. Brainard,
    United States Army.

THE OUTPOST OF THE LOST

FOREWORD

1

TWENTY-TWO white men and two Eskimos stood on
the shore and watched the sealer *Proteus* leave them,
steaming through a dark streak that ran like a river
through the surface of the ice-covered bay. The dark
streak was a "lead," as they call them in the Arctic—
a lane of water opened by the caprice of tide or wind
in the surface of a frozen sea. Leads are imperma-
nent and tricky affairs. They open and they close
without a sign of warning. A lead may remain open
for a week or it may close in an hour. There is no
telling. Yet leads are a mariner's principal depen-
dence for navigation in a frozen sea. The only other
way is to ram the ice, and, if it is not too thick, gain a
mile or so a day. But in that region of magnificent
distances, a mile in a day can be called movement

only in an academic sense. Still, there are times when a mile in a day is a great deal, and the twenty-two Americans and two Eskimos were to find it so.

But this time the lead stayed open and the *Proteus* put distance between herself and the men on shore at a rate that made no secret of Captain Pike's anxiety to separate himself from his late passengers as speedily as might be. For six fretful days his ship had lain at anchor while the passengers whom Captain Pike had brought north disembarked themselves and their belongings. Then he steamed away only to be blocked by the ice before he had made good a mariner's mile. For six days he lay there, ice-locked and helpless. On the seventh day, that is to say August 26, 1881, the lead clove a path through the ice of Lady Franklin Bay and the *Proteus* was under way and gone for good.

The twenty-four knocked off work to see her out of sight. Two of them climbed the ice-sheeted boulders of Cairn Hill for a last look. They came down in time to share the astonishment of their comrades at the sight of a man scrambling over the ice on the harbor toward them. It was Lieutenant Kislingbury. He had missed the ship.

The company was now twenty-five. Lieutenant Kislingbury took his misfortunes with a serenity common to professional soldiers of the period. The lieutenant was a big fellow of a placid and philosophic turn. He was also a late sleeper, and that was the immediate cause of his predicament. He had sailed as a member of the Lady Franklin Bay Expeditionary Force, as our company was known in the vernacular of the War Department. But from the first he did not get on so well with Lieutenant Greely, the commanding officer. The break came during the six-day delay while the ice-blocked *Proteus* was trying to get under way. Lieutenant Greely reproved him and Kislingbury asked to be relieved and sent back to the United States on the *Proteus*. Greely complied, but it took time to put all this in writing according to the somewhat leisurely I-am-sir-your-most-obedient-servant official forms of the day. It happened that this was just the time Lieutenant Kislingbury needed to catch the *Proteus*. As it was, he started over the ice too late, for the lead had opened and Captain Pike was on his way.

That evening in the chilly atmosphere of a tent pitched on the ice, a young sergeant wrote in his

diary with an arm a little stiff from swinging a ham-
mer most of the day: "We won't see anything from
the civilized world for almost a year. Perhaps not
for two years." The last sentence was a forehanded
preparation against disappointment. Sergeant Brainard expected, certainly he fondly hoped, to see the
friendly masts of the *Proteus* in Lady Franklin Bay
again next August. Also, without doubt, did Lieutenant Kislingbury, for, having been relieved of all
duty, his present status of guest was bound to become irksome long before that.

2

One year and one day later Sergeant Brainard
took pencil in hand to record the prepared-for disappointment as an accomplished fact. He let himself
down easily, but grim stuff lay between the simple
lines. "In a few days the jolly-boat *Valorous* will be
taken across Archer Fiord and left at Cape Baird for
use next year, if, once more, a relief vessel fails to
reach us and we are compelled to retreat south in our
few small boats."

The *Proteus* had not come back. For more than

two months now the twenty-five in their camp, fifteen hundred miles north of the Arctic circle, as isolated as though it were pitched on a star, had nursed what the sergeant thus obliquely concedes to have been a vain hope.   Day after day Cairn Hill had been scaled and the sea to the south swept with glasses.   The little steam launch, *Lady Greely*, (the name is a courtesy to the commanding officer's wife who had been very thoughtful of the men) had been fired up and nosed through the leads of all adjacent waters in the hope of greeting a relief ship on the way.   A hundred little plans and preparations were made and discarded.   Once the state of the sea looked so promising that the indefatigable Greely suspended all field work so that every one might be present at the station *if* a vessel should arrive.   *If* and not *when*. The little band did not permit their hopes to lead them too far.   There must be no dejection in any event.   Spirits must be kept up, ship or no ship.

Should no ship come the next year to take them off—that would be a different matter and a grave one, as the sergeant implies.   The expedition must then make its own way to civilization, in open boats and sledges over several hundred miles of wild

Arctic sea and wild Arctic ice, that had been traversed only four times in history and then with difficulty by staunch ships, including the *Proteus* that had
brought them up.

3

After all that first year had not passed disagree-
ably, and it is doubtful if any one, not excepting
Lieutenant Kislingbury, regretted the experience,
future uncertainty thrown into the bargain. The entire party had had the distinction of spending a winter farther north than any Arctic explorers had ever
wintered, with the exception of an English outfit that
had wintered on shipboard. Moreover, two of their
number had set a new Farthest North record in the
centuries old race to the Pole. In those days, to set
a new Farthest of five or ten miles was as rare a distinction as it is now to skim over the Pole itself in
an airship.

That first winter there was weather in which Medford rum froze solid and the kerosene oil had to be
thawed out before the lamps could be lighted. Private
Schneider undertook a special job of foster-mothering

some of the newly born Eskimo puppies whose parents had been picked up in Greenland on the way north. One who will try to make a pet of an Eskimo dog is entitled to credit. Eskimo dogs have the worst dispositions of any canine on earth. Mothers will eat their young. Schneider would take the pups into the men's quarters and warm them and feed them. One frisky little fellow dashed out of the door to have a look into the garbage barrel, and, to illustrate how little this young scion of Greenland ancestry knew about real cold weather, he froze solid in his tracks and had to be chopped out with an ax. The amiable Schneider warmed him up and thus averted what otherwise would have been the first casualty of the Lady Franklin Bay Expedition.

And so it went. A number of peculiar things will happen to any twenty-five men cooped up where for six or eight weeks at a stretch the temperature does not rise above the freezing-point for mercury, which is thirty-nine degrees below zero.

The party was fairly comfortably situated, nevertheless. It lived in a long, low, barrack-like house, the lumber for which had been brought up ready cut on the *Proteus*. The ready-cut lumber idea was a new one in 1881, at least to the Lady Franklin Bay people, who marveled at the progress of science and invention as they put their house together. Lieutenant Greely christened it Fort Conger, after United States Senator Conger who had sponsored the appropriation bill that provided the funds for the expedition. Fort Conger consisted of three rooms—one for the four officers, including the disengaged Kislingbury, one for the enlisted men and the Eskimos, and a kitchen. There was also a cubicle with a bathtub and a snow-melting arrangement rigged up in it, so that Saturday night was fittingly observed, for the first and perhaps the only time in the history of Arctic exploration. Years later Peary came through this part of the country and, finding Fort Conger standing in good shape, wintered there, but whether he observed Saturday night as scrupulously as Lieutenant Greely's command does not appear. Perhaps not, Peary being, by then, a seasoned polar traveler.

The Greely people were not as yet seasoned polar travelers, although most of them were familiar with hardship and with danger. They were officers and soldiers of the United States Regular Army who had volunteered for this duty and for the most part had been gathered up on short notice from regiments serving on Indian campaigns in the Far West. As the expedition was primarily a scientific one, a few husky fellows who were familiar with the instruments necessary to the required observations had been enlisted by special arrangement.

The surgeon was Dr. Octave Pavy, a Louisiana creole educated in France. Aside from Jens and Fred, the two Greenlanders employed as dog drivers, he was the only member of the party who had been in the Arctic before. The commanding officer, First Lieutenant Adolphus W. Greely, Fifth Cavalry, came from Newburyport, Massachusetts. He had been in the army since the outbreak of the Civil War when he went out as a seventeen-year-old private of Massachusetts volunteers. He was a New Englander of the traditional type, meaning the type more often found in tradition than in the flesh—tall, spare, stern, kindly and terribly conscientious. Altogether it was a rather mixed company to share the intimacy of an Arctic winter night beneath the smoky oil lamps of Fort Conger.

At first there had been plenty to do, and the work was intelligently organized by the commanding officer and tackled with zeal by the men. Provisions were stowed, and in this respect the Lady Franklin Bay Expedition fared well. Tons and tons of coal were hauled from a surface mine a few miles away. Scientific instruments were set up and sledge routes explored and rationed for the field work the following spring. But in a few weeks cold and darkness put an end to practically all the outside work except the instrument tending near the station.

The monotony of the Arctic night produces strange effects on white men. They become melancholy, sleepless and very irritable. Their pallid complexions take on a greenish tinge. It is related that a party of hunters in Spitzbergen once died from simple lack of will to live. Doctor Hall, an early American explorer, observed a rooster leap from the rail of a ship into the sea and drown himself, the doctor said, from sheer dejection.

The Lady Franklin Bay Expedition fared better than this, but there were trying times and a little excitement as well. One morning, the Eskimo Jens started off without his breakfast to walk home to Greenland, a matter of a thousand miles with a sea intervening. With some difficulty he was overtaken and brought back. Another time a careless member of the party nearly burned the house down. There was an occasional encounter with polar bears—no fatalities on either side, but several scares on both. Every diversion twenty-five minds could think of was tried out—and dropped. "Checkers are all the rage now," wrote Sergeant Brainard, the faithful diarist. "But nothing lasts like long, loud arguments. Today the subject was the relative merits of the fire departments of Chicago and New York."

Lieutenant Greely delivered lectures and organized a school. Church services were held, usually with a perfect attendance record. A practically perfect score on the sinful side was also reported by the recording secretary of the Anti-Swearing Society, which imposed a penalty of extra duty for each cuss word. After a few of the members had rolled up what amounted to virtual life sentences at the tide gage, the society dissolved. Holidays were determinedly celebrated when the party, irrespective of rank, would gather about the big stove in the enlisted men's room, try to think up stories that had not been told too often before, pass cups of fragrant rum punch and sing songs of home.

Christmas called for the grandest observance of all. Lamps were cleaned and burnished. The dingy walls were brightened with flags and guidons of the soldier's old commands at home, presenting, noted Lieutenant Greely, "a gay and lively appearance not unlike army quarters in the Far West on such occasions." The presents were laid out on the long mess-table—there was no tree because no trees grow in Grinnell Land. A great box of gifts had been brought from the States. Sergeant Rice, one of the specially enlisted men, the photographer of the expedition, acted as Santa Claus and did the job well, not overlooking to insure a good laugh on each of the officers. There were presents for all, and more than one homeless soldier roughened by the rough surface of life—hard-boiled, I believe, was the World War idiom—was touched to tears by a remembrance he had never expected. This was the work of Lieutenant Greely, and it is such little things that give us the measure of Greely. A silent and often a taciturn man, his tender heart and unfailing fairness had won for him the affection and the loyalty of his command under very difficult circumstances.

Birthdays were noticed with a gift of a quart of

rum from the general stores, which the celebrant in-
variably divided among the command. December
twenty-first was celebrated—the winter solstice,
marking the polar winter midnight when the sun begins its return march. But on the last day of February, when the sun finally reappeared for a few
moments the men had almost lost interest in it. It
had been gone for one hundred and thirty-seven days
and the brief return was no great sight, Sergeant
Brainard admits. But the sergeant looked on the
cheerful side and called it "the welcome orb, hanging just above the southern horizon, rather dim with
the appearance of something about to be born. . . .
Arctic explorers," he added, "have exaggerated the
feeling of joy experienced by men for the first time
they see the returning sun. Our men were not at all
enthusiastic. Ellis muttered that he did not care a
damn if he never saw the sun."

This lethargy did not last and almost immediately
the station hummed with activity looking toward the
spring work, the preliminaries of which had been
started the fall before. Various exploring and map-
making parties went out, and there were two "dashes"
toward the Pole, one commanded by Doctor Pavy and

one by Lieutenant Lockwood. The Lockwood party beat the best record. When the Farthest was attained the lieutenant had with him but two followers, Sergeant Brainard and Eskimo Fred.

Lockwood and Brainard made a team difficult to excel. Second Lieutenant James B. Lockwood was the beau ideal of a young officer. A member of a distinguished military family, steeped in the glamourous traditions of the profession of arms, handsome, chivalrous, intelligent—could one ask for more? He had chafed terribly under the strain of the winter's inaction and was simply bursting to be off. The sergeant made a perfect work-mate. David L. Brainard was a thorough soldier—a cavalryman of the old-time Regular Army model, and a modest young gentleman on top of it. He was, in literal fact, the schoolboy (from New York State) who, five years before, impulsively decided to join the army and see the world. He had fought Indians in the West and had been wounded in action.

Lockwood and Brainard with a party of eleven left Fort Conger on April third. They crossed the ice of Robeson Channel to Greenland and started up the Greenland coast. The temperature went to fifty below zero, a point at which it was thought that white men could not live in the open, but Lockwood pressed on, eventually dropping all of his party except Brainard and Eskimo Fred. Those left behind burrowed into the snow and established provision depots to cover the return of the lieutenant and his companions.

On May 13, 1882, Lockwood and the sergeant were stopped by a blizzard, but they had won from England a Farthest North record that British explorers had held for three hundred years. "Displayed our flags," wrote Sergeant Brainard, "wrapping them about our shoulders for protection against the raw wind. . . . Our return is replete with regrets. If we only had a few more provisions!" But Lockwood had passed the point of safety as to provisions. The three were eating only every sixteen hours, and then merely a nibble of chocolate and a cup of cold musk ox stew. But the ceremony at the Farthest had not been quite finished. "I never yet visited anywhere," wrote Brainard, "without finding 'Plantation Bitters' advertised. This, the highest explored latitude, could be no exception and on the face of the cliff, I carved the familiar characters: 'St 1860 x.' " Deciphered for the present generation the trademark reads: "Started in trade 1860 with ten dollars."

On June first, Lockwood arrived at Fort Conger, having mapped one hundred miles of hitherto unknown Greenland coast and traversed ten hundred and seventy miles in fifty-nine days. A month later the vain watch for the relief ship was set.

4

The entry for September 20, 1882, in Sergeant Brainard's journal reads as follows:

"Temperature has fallen to 4.5°.

"Frederik (the Eskimo) is celebrating his thirty-second birthday. The summer has not altered Schneider's violin repertory. He has begun the second winter with 'Over the Garden Wall.'"

The second winter was harder to bear than the first one. "Sunday, October 1," records the sergeant. "Preceding Divine Service the Commanding Officer made a short talk. He asked each member to contribute something to the enjoyment of the winter which promises to be a lonely one and suggested that acrimonious arguments be discarded."

Lieutenant Greely's suggestion appears to have had slight effect. The following day Sergeant Brainard wrote: "By direction of the Commanding Officer, the entire party was assembled in the squadroom and two orders read. One reduced Sergt. Linn to the grade of private and appointed Connell a Sergt. to fill the vacancy. The other order prohibits any enlisted man from passing beyond the station more than 500 yards without permission. No explanation was given. It is a stiff order and contributes no cheer to life in these monotonous quarters."

Three weeks later. "Ellis is celebrating his forty-second birthday. Even the birthdays, once dinner is eaten and the punch drunk, have become tiresome."

Mid-November brought a diversion in the way of some of the most colorful and scientifically interesting auroral phenomena ever observed in the North. The experts and instrument men worked night and day, but Brainard, the simple cavalryman, was not in on this. Nevertheless, he stopped work on a wall of ice blocks to record the following:

"A bright streamer sprang up from the southern horizon and gradually approached the zenith with a labored movement, which resembled spasmodic puffs of smoke arising from the stack of a working loco-motive. This was gradually dissipated and then an-other streamer darted with rapidity from the northern sky, passing through the zenith and reaching the southern horizon where it remained for several minutes glowing with an intense brilliancy. The portion 10° above the northern horizon assumed the appearance of a spiral coil, contorting itself into in-conceivable forms."

This is good description for one thing, but the sergeant improves in his record for the day follow-ing, which gives a picture of the Arctic sky in action, unsurpassed by anything on that subject that I have read elsewhere.

"We were aroused by a great commotion at 5:30 a.m. With others I rushed outside and for a moment was startled by the magnificent light and movement in the sky. As we stepped out, the vivid light so blinded Israel that he sprang back and closed the door with a bang.

" 'By heavens,' he exclaimed, 'I thought the aurora was going to strike me in the face!'

"The heavens were one luminous mass of blazing light with colors of varying blues, yellows and white.

The aurora was of no definite formation, but extended to all parts of the sky, arches, streamers and patches blending harmoniously into one huge sheet. Through an occasional opening, stars of the first magnitude could be seen shining dimly, the light of all others extinguished. At the zenith and for about 30° on either side the sheet of light was without an opening, but from the irregular edges slender pencils of light shot outward.

"The drifting, gradual changes which generally have characterized the auroras were wanting in this one. A streamer would leap from the horizon, pass through the zenith and reach the opposite horizon with the quickness of thought. Receding it appeared to swoop downward almost to the earth taking new forms, coiling and twisting convulsively like a gigantic serpent. In the northern sky there gradually appeared an intense vermilion, suggestive of a conflagration, which spread 10° above the horizon and remained for several minutes. This diminished gradually and then the aurora had passed."

As the auroras flamed and died so did interest in life in general among the lonely men in darkness at Fort Conger. None of the devices that served to

punctuate the tedium the year before were any good.
There was no snap to anything, not even the holiday
celebrations, and not until the end of January did
Lieutenant Greely amend the close-confinement order
which had worked true hardship. On Washington's
birthday, the command was too deeply in the dumps
to attempt a celebration, but Sergeant Brainard got
the colors out and hoisted them with the comment:
"This should be our last holiday in Grinnell Land."

On February 27, 1883, the sun showed itself—a
day earlier than the year before—"throwing a flood
of golden light over Discovery Harbor. Like last
year the disc was much distorted as if emerging from
embryo. More beautiful by far was the coloring of
the sky. Blue tints merged with delicate greens and
above all rich carmine predominated, although partially concealed by fleecy cirrus clouds floating along
in lazy procession." And as if to show what one
peep of the sun will do: "Lieut. Lockwood informed
me that I would accompany him in a few days to
Wrangel Bay to look over the condition of the channel in preparation for our next expedition north."
But there is a chill in the sergeant's last line. "Temperature −60.2°."

5

The last of March Lockwood, Brainard and a party set out on what was to be the crowning achievement of the expedition,—a new Farthest North,—but the "dash" was brought to an abrupt end by open water off the north Greenland shore, and the expedition was obliged to rest on the laurels Lockwood and Brainard had won for it the year previous.

It was now late in April, but there was still time for one important feat of exploration—if it could be done. This was the discovery of the Western Ocean, as the parlance of polar geographers had it in those days. This contemplated the crossing of Grinnell Land from east to west. Lieutenant Greely had led a party in this attempt the year before. They added much to the knowledge of geography of that part of the world, but they did not reach the sea on the western side. Lockwood and Brainard were picked to make another try. They succeeded, in the most dramatic piece of exploring accomplished by the Lady Franklin Bay Expedition, and stumbled into the station on May twenty-sixth, nearly helpless from snow-blindness.

Except for odds and ends the work of the expedition was complete. The success attained had surpassed expectations. In addition to tomes of new scientific data, which to this day are regarded as standard, thousands of miles of unknown territory had been explored and one-eighth of the globe circumscribed north of the eightieth parallel of latitude. The voluminous records were put in scrupulous order and just enough work continued to provide recreation and mental diversion while the party awaited the ship to take them off. The burden of every conversation was home and future plans.

Lieutenant Greely had a right to be satisfied with the work of the expedition. The imprint of his leadership was upon every achievement. He had kept a comradely feeling alive among the party, and as the time for the relief ship's arrival grew near, the little differences arising from past squabbles fell away with one exception. The exception was not the case of Lieutenant Kislingbury whose trivial quarrel with his senior officer had brought about consequences which, to say the least, seem disproportionate to the issue involved. Kislingbury had not been restored to duty, but unofficially he had made himself useful. Now that it was so nearly all over he bore his commanding officer no ill-will. ,

The solitary fleck on the sky of good-will was a feud between the commanding officer and the doctor. Between the cosmopolitan bohemian and the New England puritan, the difference in temperaments had been too great. Two years of Arctic intimacy made them frank enemies. It seemed a good thing that they were to part and go their different ways, each with his own triumph. Doctor Pavy had been a good surgeon. The health of the party had been better than it was thought possible for white men to maintain so far north, and Lieutenant Greely gave his surgeon the credit.

6

On June 17, 1883, Sergeant Brainard wrote that although "it is a few weeks too early for a relief ship we cannot keep our eyes from wandering hopefully to the south." From then on eyes were never off the southern horizon. It had been the same, of course, the year before and no ship had come, but the expedition then had another year before it in any event.

This year was a different case entirely. The party was going home, was packed up and ready. What, then, if no ship should be able to fight its way through to them? As in all military enterprises an alternative was provided in the orders governing the expedition:

"It is contemplated that the permanent station [Fort Conger] shall be visited in 1882 and 1883 by a steam sealer or other vessel. . . .

"In case such vessel is unable to reach Lady Franklin Bay in 1882, she will cache a portion of her supplies . . . at the most northerly point she attains on the east coast of Grinnell Land, and establish a small depot of supplies at Littleton Island. Notice of the locality of such depots will be left at one or all of the following places, viz: Cape Hawks, Cape Sabine, and Cape Isabella."

Thus the disappointment over the failure of a ship to appear in 1882 had been mitigated by the fact that, in any event, she was to cache rations within reach down the coast to the southward. Cape Hawks, the most northerly point where a notice might be found telling where these rations were to be located, was a little short of two hundred miles distant from Fort

Conger. Cape Isabella, the most southerly cache was over two hundred and fifty miles distant.

The orders continued:

"In case no vessel reaches the permanent station in 1882, the vessel sent in 1883 will remain in Smith Sound until there is danger of its closing by ice, and, on leaving, will land her supplies and a party at Littleton Island, which party will be prepared for a winter's stay, and will be instructed to send sledge parties up the east side of Grinnell Land. . . . Lieutenant Greely will abandon his station not later than September 1, 1883, and will retreat southward by boat until the relieving vessel is met or Littleton Island is reached," or until a sledge party from the Littleton Island base was encountered.

The orders were explicit and clear. If no ship came this year the party must conduct its own retreat, but with the promise of food stored along the route by the ship that had come north in 1882, and with the two-fold chance of meeting succor—ship or party—before reaching Littleton Island, which lies in Smith Sound just off the Greenland coast and about two hundred and fifty miles from Fort Conger.

The month of June brought no ship and the strain of waiting began to tell.

Half of July went by. No ship. The tension increased. Lieutenant Greely began active preparations for a retreat in small boats.

On July nineteenth Doctor Pavy's contract as surgeon expired and he declined to sign an engagement for another year, as the regulations of the expedition required. He was therefore placed in arrest by the commanding officer to be tried by court-martial on return to the United States. Pavy retaliated with a threat to decline to act as the expedition's surgeon, but the following day he relented and prescribed for a man who was ill.

On July twenty-fourth the state of the sea looked more hopeful for the appearance of a ship than ever before. This cheered the party considerably, but the forehanded Greely pushed his plans for an unassisted retreat, and began transferring baggage and supplies to Dutch Island in Lady Franklin Bay.

On July twenty-eighth the sea was so open that Sergeant Brainard, always as moderate in his expectations of good fortune as he was in his forebodings of evil, asked, "Why is not a vessel visible?"

On July twenty-ninth Lieutenant Greely assembled the command to announce that the retreat would begin on August seventh. But the weather and the sea remained so favorable for the approach of a ship that the men found it difficult to picture themselves retreating by small boats. And even so, such fine weather would rob the adventure of many discomforts and dangers.

"Alas! Alas!" wrote Sergeant Brainard on August fourth. The weather had changed. The sea was full of ice, carried up from the south. No ship could ever have come through it. Yet it was through such ice that Greely and his men must make their way for perhaps three hundred miles in open boats, and not a sailor among them.

August seventh brought no relief. "We are as icebound as if in the midst of the Arctic winter." The retreat was postponed.

On August eighth a twenty-mile wind was dispersing the ice. A lead began to form late in the day, however, and at eleven o'clock at night it was a mile wide. Lieutenant Greely announced that if conditions were no worse by morning the party would be off.

In the morning conditions were unchanged, and the retreat began. Two years of Arctic life had been sufficient to give Greely and his men a clear idea of the undertaking that lay before them. Their orders told them what to do with the calm assurance of one who had studied the situation on a tinted map. At best they knew the retreat to be a perilous throw and with a little ill-luck it might easily become a disastrous one.

The remainder of the narrative of the Lady Franklin Bay Expedition is from the diary of Sergeant Brainard, as he wrote it with a lead pencil from day to day. Of the twenty-five men who comprised this already noteworthy expedition none had come to the front more surely than this quiet, well-mannered young soldier. When it was all over Lieutenant Greely said of him: "Brainard was the most remarkable of a number of remarkable men of that expedition."

And not the least remarkable of the Sergeant's contributions to Arctic annals is his private journal, resurrected after many years from the depths of an old trunk where its candor could give no offense to any one immediately involved.

Throughout his diary, Sergeant Brainard uses the last names of the members of the expedition, with the exceptions of the Eskimos—Jens and Frederik.

Personnel of the Lady Franklin Bay Expedition

First Lieutenant Adolphus W. Greely, 5th Cavalry.

Second Lieutenant Frederick F. Kislingbury, 11th Infantry.

Second Lieutenant James B. Lockwood, 23rd Infantry.

Octave Pavy, Assistant Army Surgeon.

Sergeant Edward Israel, Signal Corps.

Sergeant Winfield S. Jewell, Signal Corps.

Sergeant George W. Rice, Signal Corps.

Sergeant David C. Ralston, Signal Corps.

Sergeant Hampden S. Gardiner, Signal Corps.

Sergeant William H. Cross, General Service.

Sergeant David L. Brainard, 2nd Cavalry.

Sergeant David Linn, 2nd Cavalry.

Corporal Nicholas Salor, 2nd Cavalry.

Corporal Joseph Elison, 10th Infantry.

Private Roderick R. Schneider, 1st Artillery.

Private Charles B. Henry, 5th Cavalry.

Private Maurice Connell, 3rd Cavalry.

Private Jacob Bender, 9th Infantry.

Private Francis Long, 9th Infantry.

Private William Whisler, 9th Infantry.

Private Henry Biederbick, 17th Infantry.

Private Julius Fredericks, 2nd Cavalry.

Private William A. Ellis, 2nd Cavalry.

Jens Edward, dog driver.

Frederik Thorley Christiansen, dog driver.

I

THE RETREAT

August 9th, 1883.

We are on our way. This morning the entire party with the exception of Israel, Long and myself moved over to Dutch Island. We remained behind to fetch the chronometers. At about 2:30 p.m. the Commanding Officer who had been watching from Proteus Point for a favorable opening signalled us to follow.

Long took only a portion of the dinner which he was preparing when he abandoned the station. The remainder was left on the stove. Dishes, knives, forks, spoons, etc. were left on the table unwashed. Our beds remained just as they were when we crawled out in the morning. The tank attached to the cooking range was filled with water and a fire burned in the stove. I was the last to leave the station and nailed the door securely.

The dogs, faithful fellows, were not forgotten. Ten barrels of blubber, six barrels of pork and one barrel of hard bread were overturned for their use. There were 21 grown dogs and two puppies. We were sorry to part with them, but it was a case of necessity. However, if we are compelled to return to Fort Conger this fall, they will be of incalculable benefit in retreating down the coast with sledges in the spring of 1884.

I have been assigned to the command of the large English boat *Valorous*, and Rice to the whale-boat *Narwhal*. Lieut. Greely with Lieuts. Lockwood and Kislingbury and Dr. Pavy are in the steam launch [*Lady Greely*]. Lieut. Lockwood carries a large army revolver, Lieut. Greely a sabre and a revolver, as well as his shoulder knots and helmet cord.

Directly after our arrival at Dutch Island, Lieut. Greely ordered the entire party to advance. The ice had not yet broken on the channel side of the island and our only course was toward the western entrance, between Bellot Island and Sun Cape. The ice was closing in as we started and we fought for our advance foot by foot. An unexpected bump spilled Rice overboard.

August 10th.

Reaching the western entrance, we ran into a little bight in Sun Cape where we tied up and landed for a short rest at 1 a.m. I accompanied Lieut. Greely to an eminence overlooking Lady Franklin Bay. A lane of water starting nearly at our feet extended across the bay to within three miles of the opposite shore. It was choked intermittently with broken ice and cut off from our boats by densely packed ice. Nevertheless, orders were at once given to embark.

After many narrow escapes winding through the rapidly drifting ice, we reached a large floe about half a mile from shore onto which we hauled our boats to prevent their being crushed in the ice-field. With the steam launch, we were not so fortunate since it could not be moved quickly. It was caught between two floes and severely nipped. We expected the sides of the *Lady Greely* to succumb to the enormous pressure, but she bore the strain bravely and in a few moments settled quietly down in the water.

Half of each of the two boats' crews lay down on the ice and endeavored to rest. Rice and myself with the others stayed up to watch the movement of the ice-field through thickly falling snow flakes.

Looking back our start does not seem particularly auspicious. As we paced back and forth in the storm to keep warm, the question Rice and I discussed was, "Will we ever again reach the land of our nativity?" The ice slackened off our floe slightly at 7:30 a.m. and at 8 a.m. Lieut. Greely was awakened and our boats launched. The *Lady Greely* moved forward slowly towing the other boats.

At 10 a.m. we reached a vast space of open water. A heavy swell rolled in from the north indicating the existence of more openings in our vicinity. Lieut. Greely, however, did not think the lane was continuous and landed Lieut. Lockwood and Connell to ascertain the extent. In the meantime the twelve man sledge was ordered out to be lashed in case it should be needed to convey the boats across the floe to which we were tied. This would have meant abandoning the steam launch. Fortunately Lieut. Lockwood and Connell returned in a short time reporting the lane continuous to the opposite shore.

A high storm prevailed during the greater part of the run across the bay and Fredericks [not to be confused with Frederik, the Eskimo], as usual, contributed freely his offerings to Neptune. The depot at

Cape Baird was reached at 2 p.m. I was assigned to superintend the loading of provisions. Elison, meantime, made extensive repairs on the boats. Connell was given command of the English ice-boat stored here and the crews sub-divided.

During the evening the wind died away and the sea was smooth, except for a gentle heaving of the surface. The crews retired for a short time. Breakfast was dispatched at 11 p.m. and half an hour later we steamed out of the little harbor bidding adieu forever to the shores of Lady Franklin Bay. With the supplies picked up here we now carried fifty days rations with caches ahead of us at Carl Ritter Bay and Cape Collinson.

As we pulled out from Cape Baird, Lieut. Greely became much excited and used language toward me which my conduct did not deserve. We were all surprised by his extensive vocabulary and the fluent and forceful manner in which he delivered himself. In a moment, though, he calmed down.

A short distance from Cape Lieber we were stopped by the pack and took shelter behind the grounded floebergs which line the shore. A watch was set and the remainder of the crews retired.

August 11th.

I went on the first watch of two hours, followed by Rice who, in turn, was relieved by Connell. Lieut. Greely visited the hill at 7:45 a.m. to inspect the ice in Hall Basin. He saw the pack moving with the tide, leaving an opening along shore which would permit us to leave our uncomfortable position. He signalled to us to proceed and in an instant everything was bustle and activity. Half-clad men with unrolled sleeping bags rushed for the boats and cooking utensils, guns, etc. were loaded hurriedly.

The boats had grounded with the rapidly falling tide, but willing hands lightened the loads and without confusion we were afloat once more at 8:30. Passing through a clear channel near shore we took on the C.O. from a projecting ledge of rocks.

From the cache at Cape Cracroft we took the corned beef and then proceeded southward through the channel, closely hugging the shore. In the vicinity of Cape Defosse, the ice closed in suddenly and our boats were pushed against the ice-foot, narrowly escaping demolishment by the fearful pressure. They were unloaded, hauled up on the beach and the party went into camp at 11:20 p.m.

During the day we have passed many icebergs, the upper surfaces of which were acres in extent. I think this is something unusual for Kennedy Channel, as it has been supposed generally that no icebergs were found north of Cape Lawrence. Sergt. Rice and Long who went down to the coast, report the ice moving back and forth with the tide and packed so closely there is no hope of escape for the present.

SUNDAY, *August 12th.*

The watch reported the ice opening near shore and we pushed off at 9:15 a.m. We worked along slowly until 3 p.m. when the ice closed in and we were compelled to haul up our boats. I went on watch and from the summit of a lofty berg I soon had the pleasure of observing the ice move out gradually from shore to the southward. We took advantage of the opening instantly and our little fleet steamed down the coast through comparatively clear water.

We had gone little more than a mile when we encountered a dense pack driven northward by high wind. There was no alternative but to seek the adjacent land for protection.

At 8:20 p.m. the watch again reported the ice

opening. We hastily jumped into our boats and moved down the coast at a good rate of speed. Halted at 9:35 p.m. at Carl Ritter Bay to take on the small cache of provisions landed in 1881 from the *Proteus*. The weather has grown very disagreeable with thick fog, flying snow and a fierce wind. We are chilled to the bone.

August 13th.

Had a fine run during the night through water almost free of ice, but at 1:35 a.m. when about three miles south of Cape Leopold Von Buch, the pack compelled us to haul up our boats. The weary party immediately retired.

I went on watch at 8 a.m. and with the small boat made a trip about half a mile from shore to a large iceberg which appears to be the keystone of the pack. No opening appeared. On a second trip about two hours later I found a narrow lane close under the berg. Lieut. Greely at once ordered a start.

We passed quickly about the berg and into the open space beyond, where the pack soon closed in on our boats. Snow began falling and the weather turned cold. Nearly all the sails are used to cover the stores in the boats. Since we have no tents, we crawled under the over-hanging edges of rocks for shelter. We were wet and cold. If our feelings were bitter and our words not particularly pleasant do not blame us!

At 4:45 p.m. Whisler reported a lane along shore. It was at once taken advantage of, but the ice closed down on us very soon. We fought long to extricate ourselves, butting and charging full speed at the weak points with the *Lady Greely*; but we could make no headway.

A young seal which Lieut. Kislingbury killed was prepared for supper. I never remember eating a more delicious meal.

The ice appears closely packed along shore to the south.

August 14th.

We are helpless! Nothing has been done today. The ice changed considerably just outside of our position and much stream ice was observed flowing down the channel with the currents and tides; but this had no effect on our situation. The boats are in a protected indentation, but are gradually being impris-

oned by ice cakes. A high northerly wind has blown
all day; at 9 p.m. changed to southwest.

I saw a lane extending from Cape Lawrence
diagonally across the channel to the Greenland coast.
A ship could have bored her way through the slack
ice with ease, but small craft like ours would have
been swallowed instantly.

The water in our breaker [keg] was frozen last
night, although sitting within three feet of the *Lady
Greely's* boiler. By a meridian altitude, Israel determined our position to be in latitude 80° 44′.

Franklin Island looms up through the hazy atmosphere opposite us. The historical Cape Constitution
of Kane also rises grandly from the sea. Crozier
Island is far to the south, more diminutive than its
solitary companion, Franklin.

August 15th.

The temperature which has been ranging from 30°
to 24° fell last evening to 21° and ice two inches thick
formed. The northwest wind did not continue long,
but veered to the northeast. I volunteered to proceed
down the coast to Cape Lawrence, hoping to communicate with the vessel which may now be anchored

in Rawlings Bay awaiting an opportunity to advance to our relief. I dislike to remain inactive. Lieut. Greely, however, does not consider it advisable to separate the party.

The ice loosened somewhat at high tide and the launch was worked out about 400 yards and anchored to a grounded berg. The boats were also moved out a short distance. To accomplish this we had to work for over four hours in the ice and water, getting our feet wet and our clothing covered with ice.

While changing the position of the launch, some of the men informed me that Cross had been tampering with the fuel alcohol. I found him very much intoxicated. The Commanding Officer relieved Cross from the engine and placed Fredericks in charge.

Lieut. Greely believes that he would have been south of Cape Lawrence now had he abandoned the launch when we were first frozen in, and placed our boats and supplies on the drifting ice and floated with them southward. His idea is certainly a most extraordinary one.

Fredericks says that had the boiler of the *Lady Greely* been neglected a few minutes longer it would have been useless, whether it exploded or not.

[A note by General Brainard:

Nearly fifty years having elapsed since the rescue of the remnants of the Greely Expedition, it seems pertinent that an incident of the boat journey from Fort Conger to Cape Sabine should be made of record. The incident occurred August 15, 1883.

Lieutenant Greely had mentioned two or three times that it might be advisable, in order to facilitate our progress southward, to place the party and our equipment on the floe when it was moving with the tide, and thus gain time and distance, rather than remain inactive, beset by ice. His views were not approved generally by the party, except perhaps by Lieutenant Lockwood who was willing to risk almost anything rather than remain inactive.

Lieutenant Kislingbury, Doctor Pavy and Sergeant Rice approached me with a most extraordinary proposition to the effect that Doctor Pavy, as the only medical officer present, would announce as his professional opinion that Lieutenant Greely was too ill to continue the leadership of the expedition, and that Lieutenant Kislingbury, by virtue of his rank, would assume command. My support was asked.

I promptly declined to take part in any such plan

and told them that any division of authority, in such a crisis, would result in the destruction of the expedition. Moreover, I had sufficient confidence in the men of the party to feel that any attempt to depose Lieutenant Greely from the leadership would be resisted. The plan was dropped, but reference to it was made from time to time by the chief actors, who never quite gave up the idea.]

August 16th.

The weather remains much the same as it was yesterday—cold, cloudy and disagreeable. Winter, we may say, has already begun. The mountain tops are covered with snow, the flowers have disappeared and the short lived plants bear traces of the visitation of Jack Frost.

August 17th.

The first beautiful morning since leaving home. Home! To speak of Fort Conger as home!

With the return of the sun this morning, the spirits of the party revived. They forgot their sufferings of the last few days and new hopes rose.

The report from the hill is that open water is visible
on the Greenland coast as far south as the eye can
penetrate the hazy atmosphere. In this there is a
small ray of hope. The manner in which the men
meet this detention is beyond all praise. Not a mur-
mur escapes their lips.

The Commanding Officer reiterates his determination to put the boats on a floe and drift to Littleton
Island. The scheme sounds like madness. If my
opinion is asked, I will object. The experiences of
the *Hansa*, of the *Polaris* and other expeditions have
demonstrated the unreliability of such cheap methods
of transportation.

If we cannot proceed by the fifth of September, a
cache of our remaining provisions should be made
and the whole party retreat to Fort Conger where
until November 15th we can hunt game and haul coal
for our winter's use. Enough stores remain to enable
us to live until next spring. An excellent line of retreat might then be conducted down the coast to Littleton Island with sledges. The provisions which we
place in the cache here could then be used to advantage.

Proceeding as we are now, we are basing our
hopes on the assumption that a ship has succeeded

in passing the barriers of Melville Bay and is now awaiting us. What will become of this party of poor shivering wretches on reaching Littleton Island at the beginning of winter with nothing to subsist on, if the ship is not there? The question is not a pleasant one to contemplate. On a retreat judiciously conducted during the spring months, we could defy cold, hunger and death which ever dogs the footsteps of the weary Arctic traveller.

[As it turned out, there was almost uncanny wisdom in this reasoning of Sergeant Brainard. As he made his speculations the relief ship of 1883 which they were daily hoping to meet, or at worst to find at Littleton Island, was actually at the bottom of Kane Sea and had been there for nearly a month. She was the *Proteus*, the ship that had brought the expedition to Grinnell Land in 1881. But this time she had not been so fortunate in her fight with the ice. Passing the barriers of Melville Bay, steaming past Littleton Island in Smith Sound, which she expected to visit on her way back in case she did not connect with Greely beforehand, she had gained Bache Island in the Kane Sea, about three hundred miles from Lady Franklin Bay. There a lead closed on her, crushing her sides as if they were so much paper, and she sank within a few hours on July twenty-third, sixteen days before Greely and his men had started their retreat. All of which the Greely band were to learn ere long, as they were to learn also the history of the relief ship of 1882 which was to cache food along the coast. The command was now approaching the northernmost of the three points where this food, or notice of its location, might be found.]

August 18th.

At midnight Israel who was on watch reported a lane starting two miles below camp and extending northward past our position. I went with the Commanding Officer in the small boat to a large floeberg about 200 yards from the launch, and observed that the water was gradually encroaching in our direction.

At the same time Lieut. Kislingbury reported from the hill large spaces of open water on the Greenland coast. The surface of the pool which had just opened near us was as clear and placid as a polished mirror and reflected in its depths the hills which line the shore. A beautiful picture, but how deceptive!

We made strenuous efforts to reach this pool, but

it closed when we were yet far away. To add to our discomfort snow began falling and S.W. winds freshened. A favorable lane appeared at 9 p.m. We worked the launch into open water and taking the boats in tow again started southward, vastly relieved to be free. We have been locked in by the ice for five days.

SUNDAY, *August 19th.*

We reached a small bay about six miles from Cape Lawrence at 3:40 a.m. when the tide changed and closed our lead. The ice came charging down on our frail boats with the speed of a race-horse and we barely escaped to a small harbor which was protected by several grounded floebergs. I never saw ice move with greater rapidity. Within two minutes after we had left the open pool, the surface was covered with a convulsive mass which would have ground our boats to atoms.

We had travelled about ten miles. The cook served coffee and all hands, except the watch, turned in for a few hours rest.

At 10 a.m. we were aroused by a report from Connell that a lane extended across the entrance to the bay. We steamed for about three miles and then a blind lead ran us into the drifting pack. After more than two hours of hard labor, during which time we were carried forward a mile, we worked into shore and tied up.

The cook prepared supper and the Commanding Officer read a Psalm. He then gave me orders to proceed with Eskimo Fred to Cape Lawrence to learn of the condition of the ice there. We set out trudging wearily along through the deep snow and over broken rocks, the sharp edges cutting our boots.

August 20th.

As we travelled, a dense fog came up from the south, passed up the channel and disappeared as quickly as it had appeared. A southerly gale drove the ice from shore leaving an excellent lane which we could have navigated without difficulty in a ship.

Reached Cape Lawrence at 3:15 a.m. and found the Smith Sound pack stretching across the channel from Cape Lawrence toward Cape Jackson, unbroken and impenetrable. Nothing was seen in Rawlings Bay. With heavy hearts we turned back.

The launch and boats ran up nearly to Cape Lawrence where the lane ended. Lieut. Greely went ahead a short distance and from a slight elevation saw the lane again opening. We moved up Rawlings Bay and anchored to await a change in tide.

August 21st.

We arrived at Cape Wilkes at 1 a.m. and found the ice closely pressed on shore and further advance cut off. The small Whitehall boat which has been leaking badly for several days, was broken up for fuel and the fragments stowed away in the other boats. The weather is damp, foggy and disagreeable.

On the change of tide, the ice cleared away from shore toward the south, but the eddying currents at the cape drifted it in again. A start was ordered at 9:40 a.m. and within ten minutes, our boats were nipped between the ice-foot and the pack. Only the desperate exertions of the party saved them. The whaleboat, commanded by Rice, was badly damaged although he did everything in his power to protect her. The *Lady Greely* was also nipped.

We are watching anxiously for a ship, our only salvation. We have crossed the Rubicon and to turn back now is out of the question. We *must* advance although I am fearful it will result in another Franklin disaster. [Sir John Franklin with one hundred and twenty-eight men sailed from England in 1845 in search of the Northwest Passage. Three years later, after valuable discoveries in the Arctic, the whole expedition had perished, although its fate remained a mystery for fifteen years. Treacherous ice first had taken its toll in men and boats. Those who survived these adventures later starved to death.]

At 1 p.m. the tide having slackened the ice from shore we ran across Richardson Bay reaching the opposite coast near Cape Collinson at 5 p.m. I was directed to proceed to the cape to examine the English cache. I found it without difficulty, but many of the stores were missing. Bears evidently had broken into the packages.

August 22nd.

A southwest gale opened the ice slightly and we ran across to Cape Collinson where we halted long enough to secure the provisions. At the northern cape of Joiner Bay, the steersman ran the launch into an iceberg and the shock broke a steam-cock. We were detained an hour for repairs.

The run across Joiner Bay was made quickly. The ice would not permit our passing around the cape and at 8:55 a.m. we tied up to the ice-foot on the south side near the entrance.

In a few minutes, though, the ice moved out leaving a narrow passage near shore which enabled us to round Cape McClintock where an excellent harbor was found. Not until 3 p.m. did the ice loosen and then we ran across Scoresby Bay. About one mile south of Cape Norton Shaw our lane closed and we tied up to the nearest ice-foot.

Lieut. Greely sent Rice for an observation. He reports the ice closely packed to the south and no water anywhere visible.

This has been a cold, disagreeable day with a storm—half rain, half snow.

August 23rd.

I have never spent a more disagreeable night. Snow, mixed with rain, fell all night saturating our clothing, sleeping bags and other property. At an early hour we dropped down to Cape John Barrow and tied up.

I was on the hill watching the ice when the pack

came bearing down on our frail boats. I held my breath expecting in another moment to see them in splinters. But our party was equal to the occasion. Rice found a small hole in the ice-foot into which he ran his boat. The steam launch was not so fortunate, but escaped with a few scratches. The other boats were sheltered behind a berg.

At 3 p.m. the ice opened somewhat and we proceeded a short distance south when we again met the pack. Lieut. Greely forced his way into it and tied up to a floe. We are drifting out into the channel, slightly northward.

August 24th.

At 6 a.m. the ice loosened and we passed through to the coast. It was with a feeling of relief that we again placed our feet on firm, unyielding soil. The boats were tied up and I was ordered to inspect the ice. From Cape Frazier it appears closely packed to the southward.

I returned late at night and learned that the boats had been secured in a fine little harbor after having suffered greatly in an exposed position. The whale-boat was stove in.

Rain has been falling for hours and we are drenched.

August 25th.

Our sufferings were alleviated somewhat by the cessation of the rain at midnight. The ice opened at 4:40 a.m. and we immediately started. Cape Frazier where the two tides meet, was rounded without difficulty, but in Gould Bay the packed ice stopped our advance. Beyond our position, however, stream ice could be seen and a little patient waiting rewarded us. We proceeded another half mile, tying up to a grounded floeberg.

Frederik shot a small seal which I afterward divided. Great interest is always taken in these divisions. When killed the seals are cut into small pieces in order that each of our three messes will be given its proportion of the best parts. The pieces are then thrown into three piles from which choice is made by lot.

Our daily ration since leaving Fort Conger has been one pound of meat and the same of bread. Beans and potatoes are used alternately at the rate of two ounces per day. Fruits, such as cranberries

and apples, are issued occasionally. Tea and coffee
are our drinks. We have cooked with wood taken
from the small boat and barrels collected at different
caches.

For a short time this morning, our despondency
was changed into hopefulness by the appearance of
the sun. It is quite remarkable what effect the sun
has on our spirits. However, a dense fog remained
with us during the greater part of the day.

While waiting for something to turn up, a water
space suddenly appeared to the south. The fog
interfered greatly with our progress, however, and
also we were afraid that the relief ship might pass
us. In order to avert anything like this, Schneider
stood in the bow of the *Valorous* and blew vigorously
at intervals of two minutes on a large tin horn.

SUNDAY, *August 26th.*

Reached Cape Hawks in comparatively clear water.
With considerable difficulty the cache of English provisions was found. The greater part of the bread
was mouldy and some of it entirely spoiled. The
other articles were 168 pounds of dried potatoes,
three gallons of rum and one keg of onion pickles.

[The English cache was an old one, left years before by a British party. It was news of (and food from) the relief ship of 1882 that the party sought and expected at Cape Hawks, but neither was found either at Hawks or its environs. This, however, did not necessarily mean that the relief expedition of 1882 had been a failure. Cape Hawks was the farthest north of three points where rations were to be left. The next one down the coast was Cape Sabine. The party headed for it.]

Rice who had been dispatched to Washington Irving Island to examine the cairn for records returned with the report that it had not been visited since 1881 when we passed up the coast. He left a brief record of our retreat from Conger. Rice reported the ice in favorable condition for navigation by a ship to Cape Sabine. But why does the ship not come? Since no record was found at Washington Irving Island I do not believe a relief vessel has been able to approach this far north since the *Proteus* made the trip with our party. Perhaps, even now, the ship we await is lost in Melville Bay or in the pack. A naval vessel, if sent, would not dare to enter this ice, despite Rice's report. If not lost, perhaps the vessel is awaiting us at Littleton Island. I trust so—if we are able to get there.

We started at 4 p.m., Rice being assigned to steer the launch. He proved the most skillful of any at the tiller yet. The coast was abandoned and our course shaped directly for Cape Sabine which is distinctly visible.

August 27th.

The boats were firmly frozen into the floe this morning. What we have feared for so long has happened. In the words of a navigator, we are beset. The ice-pack completely encloses us. I doubt that the boats can be extricated, although our little party, as usual, continue to live in hope. The retreat, I believe, will have to be reorganized, our boats abandoned, and escape effected on foot over the floe when the ice becomes firmer. I do not think that ever before did an exploring party meet with as many adversities as we have on this retreat. We have managed to travel southward about 200 miles, but actually we have gone 400 miles to get here. Winter has set in extraordinarily early. Jens said this morning that had we been able to advance one mile farther yesterday to the open water seen in the distance, we would have had no difficulty in proceeding southward. Rice who was steering the *Lady Greely,* is of the same opinion.

By astronomical observations, Israel has determined our position to be in latitude 79° 22′ north; longitude 73° 30′ 11″ west. The ice appears to have a slight northerly movement today. Naturally we drift as tide and current decree.

As the date of our escape from the pack is a matter of conjecture, if at all, I asked Lieut. Greely whether I could reduce the rations slightly. He would not accede to my request, fearing that such action would have a depressing effect on the men.

We rigged a tripod on the floe this evening and placed a flag to signal the relief vessel which is our main hope of escape now. The tripod can be climbed about fifteen feet and makes an excellent lookout. If there were only something to be seen in the distance!

On a small paleocrystic floe near our boats we found a small pool of fresh water. This is a piece of good fortune for it will allow us to economize on our fuel.

A clear, beautiful evening. The temperature fell to 12.5° at 11 p.m.

[Sergeant Brainard is so temperate in his statements, so disinclined to dramatize or emphasize the dangers he and his comrades are in, that the reader may not grasp the precise significance of what has occurred. The boats of the party are frozen fast, mere specks in the polar ice-pack, which is constantly in motion under the influence of winds, currents, temperature and tides. A more perilous position would be difficult to imagine. The pack may do anything. It may heave up an ice mountain under their feet, precipitating boats and men into the sea beneath. It may break up into a series of small ice cakes floating in separate directions, taking half of the party one way and half another. A variety of things may happen, and do happen during the thirty-four days, any hour of which might have been their last, that they were to spend on cakes of drifting ice, trusting to the chance of events to bring them to land— somewhere.]

August 28th.

The pack moved slightly to the north and east during the night. A southerly motion has also been detected. Both probably are due to the change of tides. A decided drift toward the south was observed when the tide was flood. This is slightly to our advantage, but I doubt that the tide is sufficient to carry us any distance south.

Adversity in its worst form would not dampen the spirits of our men. Our situation is desperate. At any moment this ice may crumble from beneath us and swallow the entire party. Still, while exercising this evening they danced and sang as merrily as if in their own comfortable homes.

August 29th.

The drift south continues, but the movement is so slow that it is not perceptible without bearings. Israel estimated the distance drifted at three miles. We are perhaps eighty miles from Littleton Island where a boat may await us. The island is east of our position. The tendency of the drift is toward the south and west.

Lanes opened in the direction of Cape Prescott

this morning, but we were unable to get into them. Our time is passed principally in reading, sleeping and eating. The sergeants, each in turn, take tours of two hours to watch the movement of the ice. The others perform no duties except that of cooking. Snow about twenty inches deep covers the floe.

Early this morning Jewell saw a fox prowling about the boats. They must earn a very precarious living in these barren ice-fields.

August 30th.

The drift from midnight until 10 a.m. was about one mile to northeast. We then turned and drifted southwest one and two-tenths miles, making our gain for today one-fifth of a mile. The minimum temperature last night was 11.8°. No Polar party has ever before recorded a temperature so low in August.

Numerous water spaces are visible to the north and east of our camp. Dark clouds overhang the southern horizon, indicating abundance of water in that direction. In fact, the pack seems concentrated around our party as if determined to crush us within its mighty grasp. With the indications of water to the south, I am willing to accept Rice's and Jen's view that we could have proceeded to safety if the pack had allowed us one more mile. But, then, that great misfortune is in line with the ill-luck which has been ours from the start of the retreat.

I took an inventory of provisions this evening and found fifty-five days supplies on hand.

Lieut. Greely informs me that he will start with sledges and boats for Littleton Island as soon as the ice will permit. Everything not absolutely useful to us or in the least cumbersome will be abandoned here on the floe.

August 31st.

The day opened cloudy with a light northwest wind. Rain fell this evening. We hastily improvised shelters which served as a partial protection. The Commanding Officer tried to soften our misery with an issue of rum.

Israel estimated the distance drifted south in the last twenty-four hours at three miles.

September 1st.

We are still drifting slowly southward.

In the early afternoon the northern ice pack came charging down on our unprotected floe breaking like sticks the ice which offered opposition, and heaping

it in great, quivering, groaning masses about us.
The relentless pressure opened wide seams in the
floe on which we are camped. Our boats were hauled
up without a moment to spare. The *Lady Greely*
could not be handled so quickly and was severely
nipped. She did not succumb completely as we had
expected, but rose grandly as the pressure increased
and stood high above the water in a cradle formed
by the grinding ice. At 6:30 p.m. when the tide
turned and the pressure was removed, she settled
down into the water gradually. At 11 p.m. she sustained another nip from a sudden movement and, as
on the former occasion, she rose nobly and remained
uninjured.

Our two natives—Jens and Eskimo Fred—each
killed a seal today. A good natured spirit of rivalry
exists between them. I suspect that Fred whose blood
has been mingled with the Danes often takes advantage of Jens. As an incentive, a drink of rum is
given the fortunate hunter.

No portion of the seal is ever wasted. Even the
blood is now considered a luxury. If drunk when
warm, it is very palatable—not unlike raw eggs in
flavor.

SUNDAY, *September 2nd.*

Our southerly drift since yesterday has been estimated at over three miles. The launch was lifted
frequently by the pressure of the ice today, but no
injuries at any time. Our floe which is of one season's growth only is slowly being crumbled beneath
us by the tremendous pressure from the northern
pack.

An opportunity occurred last evening to change
our position, but it was not taken advantage of. I
think this was unwise since we could have moved a
few yards to another floe which is larger and thicker.
It would probably withstand the effects of a gale and
we feel very uncertain about the strength of our
young floeberg.

The barometer is falling rapidly.

September 3rd.

On rising for breakfast this morning we were much
surprised to observe the remarkable progress our
floe had made during the night and early morning
while fog obscured the coast. From compass sights
it was found that we had drifted two miles north in
four hours with the flood tide.

Sharp comments made by Lieut. Kislingbury on our present inactivity were overheard and objected to by the Commanding Officer. Lieut. Greely directed me to summon Lieuts. Lockwood and Kislingbury, the Doctor and Rice for a consultation. I was also directed to be present.

Lieut. Kislingbury advised that we abandon the launch and the *Valorous* and, taking the two remaining boats, move from floe to floe across the intervening space to Albert Head, thence across Buchanan Strait; in any case, to start tomorrow or as soon thereafter as possible. Dr. Pavy concurred in this plan.

Lieut. Lockwood thought it desirable to get to shore as quickly as possible, but was not prepared to pass judgment for final action. I did not advise a movement in the present unsettled state of the pack, but would wait until the end of the month or until the floe had cemented sufficiently for travelling over it with our heavy loads. Meantime we are slowly drifting south. The recommendations made by Rice were substantially the same as mine. As a result of the conference, the Commanding Officer decided to wait here until the new ice has cemented.

Whisler was discharged and reenlisted today.

September 4th.

Our floe continues to drift slowly south. Snow has fallen all day. We constructed a tepee into which can be crowded sixteen of the men. The other nine will be accommodated in Connell's boat over which a shelter has been placed.

Jens shot a seal.

While on duty this evening, I saw a small lane opening in the ice. I reported at once to Lieut. Greely and the party was aroused. Made one and one-quarter miles when the lane ended. We hauled our boats onto a paleocrystic floe and all except the watch retired at 11 p.m. We had to tow the launch during the greater part of the distance because the fan [propeller] had been displaced yesterday while she was subjected to the terrible pressure from the pack.

One more instant of our ill-luck.

Cross and Elison began to work on two sledges with which, in addition to the large English sledge, we will endeavor to escape from this inhospitable floe. The seats in the steam launch will be sacrificed for sledge runners and barrel staves will be used as cross-ties.

September 5th.

A beautiful bright day.

At breakfast we were abreast of Victoria Head. At dinner we were a long distance south of it. Strange as it may seem, we drifted in a southerly direction during the flood tide when we should have been drifting north. We have drifted six miles in two days. Light southerly winds have prevailed all day.

I placed our flag on the long pole and have planted it firmly in the ice on the summit of our floe.

I continue to marvel at the conduct of the men since our besetment. When we were first caught by the pack, I thought there would be lamentations without end, but to my surprise matters are just the opposite. Good-natured chaff, a hearty ringing laugh and the snatch of a song are heard at almost any time.

September 6th.

The large iceberg which has been our constant companion and protector for several days is now bearing down on our floe and likely to prove itself a treacherous friend.

September 7th.

A gale since midnight has accelerated our drift and at the same time pushed us in toward the land. We passed abreast of Cape Albert this morning at a distance of not more than four miles. At noon we were in latitude 79° 0.6′, a drift of six and three-tenths miles during the last 24 hours.

September 8th.

The day dawned bright, clear and calm. Stars were seen last night for the first time since spring. The light was uncertain at midnight. Our latitude is the same as yesterday.

Connell encountered a walrus sporting in a pool not far from our floe. He fired eight shots, but the bullets glanced from his skull as if fired against a rock.

The temperature fell last night to −0.8°, something quite unkown at this period of the year. Ice is forming rapidly about us. The pools are all covered and the floe will soon be cemented together so that travelling will be feasible. At the suggestion of Lieut. Greely I had the sledges lashed together.

Lieut. Greely says he will abandon the *Lady*

Greely and *Valorous* and taking the other two boats to carry our supplies, try to reach land in the vicinity of Cocked Hat Island.   He intends starting day after tomorrow.   I am going out with Eskimo Fred tomorrow to look for a sledge road through the broken surface of the pack, toward land and liberty.   I expect it to be rather dangerous duty, but somehow the presence of the faithful Frederik gives one a certain feeling of security.

The ice in Buchanan Strait does not appear to have broken up this year.   If we are not deceived in our observations, it is no wonder—no longer a mystery— the ship did not reach us.

SUNDAY, *September 9th.*

Nothing has been done today owing to bad weather.   Lieut. Greely again held a consultation with the same officers and non-commissioned officers as before and, as a result, has decided to start for land tomorrow.

September 10th.

Owing to a snow-storm we were unable to start until the afternoon.   Meantime, the *Lady Greely* and the

Valorous were dismantled and abandoned. A record of our retreat from Fort Conger was left in each in case they should be picked up by the relief vessel. The main mast of the *Valorous* was placed in position and from its top a signal flag was left fluttering.

The Commanding Officer called us together to say that if the party so desired the pendulum would be abandoned because it is so heavy. The value of our observations in the Arctic rests with subsequent comparative observations to be made from this same pendulum. The men appreciate this important fact and to their credit not one would hear of abandoning the pendulum.

When we started I went ahead to select the road, turning back after having traversed about a mile to assist on the sledges. The hauling was exceedingly heavy and the men were straining with every ounce of their energy. Nowhere was there a level stretch of ice—all rubble and small bergs which had been smashed and crumbled by the pack.

The small ice-boat, *Beaumont*, and about 700 pounds of stores were taken on the twelve man sledge. Following came the two small sledges, one carrying about two thousands pounds and the other sixteen hundred. Both broke down a few minutes after starting. In the second load were the whale-boat, baggage, stores, etc. The third comprised the remainder of our property—oars, ammunition, arms, provisions, etc. Altogether we were hauling about sixty-five hundred pounds.

Each load had to be advanced alternately with all hands in the drag ropes. The officers worked along with us. We travelled five miles to make good only one mile. Camped on the floeberg at 7:15 p.m.

We are about eleven miles from land. If the wind continues favorable our ice-raft will remain almost stationary or else carry us southwest toward our destination. On the other hand, with unfavorable wind, we may expect to be carried out to sea.

An issue of rum tonight.

September 11th.

Notwithstanding disagreeable weather we started with the first load at 8:40 a.m. I again went ahead to select and prepare a road for the heavily laden sledge. Excessive thirst attends the severe labor of the sledgers, but fortunately numerous pools are to be found on the paleocrystic floes.

After we had advanced about a mile and a quarter, a heavy snow-storm warned us that it was not prudent to proceed further and we camped on a paleocrystic floe of great extent. The large sledge made three trips, or six trips for the men in the drag ropes.

At the southern limit of the floeberg is a large grounded iceberg which Lieut. Greely directed me to visit and note the travelling conditions in that direction. The Doctor accompanied me. Climbing to the summit of the berg, we could see a great expanse of new ice studded here and there with small rubble. This ice is not strong enough to bear the weight of our sledges. While standing on the berg, a school of walruses came to the surface breaking through the ice with their heads.

Our outlook is dismal. The party could never reach land over this thin ice. It was the opinion of the Doctor and myself that nothing could be done at present to alter our position, except to move south to the edge of the floe and await the action of the spring tides which come in four days. Perhaps they will strengthen the floe and then we will be able to pass over it in safety.

On our return the Commanding Officer again held

a consultation and the Doctor and I made our report
and recommendations. The general wish was to remain where we are until after the spring tides. If
the ice holds together, it will be strong enough to
travel over. If the tides break the ice, we may be
able to embark in our boats and reach land.

The Commanding Officer favors travelling southeast toward Greenland by a series of floes which he
thinks extend in that direction. He has directed Rice
to make a trip of eight hours duration in that direction tomorrow to ascertain the prospects.

September 12th.

Rice returned soon after noon to report the travelling good. We at once prepared for a move.

On the recommendation of the officers, Rice and
myself, the Commanding Officer ordered the whale-
boat abandoned. The sledge has been broken and
daily growing weaker under the great weight of the
boat. In a few days, it would have been useless.
Such a calamity would be a fatal blow for without
this sledge we are helpless. We left a record of our
fortunes and misfortunes in the boat and nailed a
signal flag to an oar.

After two miles we reached the edge of the floe where our first load was deposited. The others were brought up later.

A wide crack at the edge of this floe does not argue well for the work tomorrow.

September 13th.

A bright, beautiful morning. The crack did not prove troublesome, except to Bender who fell in. The first load was started at 7:55 a.m. Jens and I went ahead to select the route. We traversed seven and a half miles to make good one and a half miles. The new ice is thin and dangerous.

September 14th.

The roar of the moving and grinding pack east of us in the axis of the channel is something so terrible that even the bravest cannot appear unconcerned. To add to the scene of desolation, dark portentous clouds hang over the horizon to remind us that our floe is not connected with the land, but drifting helplessly in Kane Sea. The small sledge broke down while crossing a band of rubble ice, necessitating an extra trip with the large sledge.

Made good one and a half miles. But we did not keep this hard-earned gain for long. Just before we reached camp with the last load a southerly gale came up. In the last few hours we have drifted back north losing more than twice the distance we worked so hard to gain. We are still drifting northward and morning will undoubtedly find us many miles at sea.

September 15th.

We have drifted northeast all night under the influence of the gale. Cape Camperdown is nearly north of us. Israel's observations yesterday placed us in latitude 78° 55′ north. Today our position was 79° 01.8′, nearly seven miles of our dearly earned ground lost. We are even many miles north of where we abandoned the launch and with no prospect of regaining what we have lost. We continue northeastward, drifting in the sea on a piece of ice of uncertain texture. We do not know what to expect from the Polar Pack. Too much pressure will shatter the floeberg and too little will leave us open to the danger of drifting into collision with an iceberg.

The gale subsided at 4 p.m. and our position by bearings shows that we have now lost fifteen miles.

SUNDAY, *September 16th.*

With the gale past the direction of our drift again
has changed to the south. Our floeberg at noon was
in the midst of the Polar Pack in latitude 79° 0.7′, a
drift of 1.1 miles since last evening in the face of
adverse tides and winds. The currents here apparently have a strong southerly tendency.

Rice and Jens went out this morning to inspect the
ice. On returning they reported just what we expected—it is impracticable for sledging.

A council again was called this evening. Dr. Pavy
insisted that the only sure method of escape is to
push forward at once over the broken pack to Cape
Sabine where a cairn and cache of provisions from
the relief vessel are supposed to await us. The
others, including myself, recommended no move until after the spring tides which now are at their
highest. The floe will then take some definite direction. The Commanding Officer again expressed himself willing to abandon the pendulum whenever any
member of the party should announce himself as dis-
satisfied with hauling it. We are unanimous that it
should be kept as long as possible.

I took an inventory of the provisions and found

that at least forty days full rations remained. The hunters were out on the ice all day in search of game. They saw bear tracks and a small seal in a pool near camp. Frederik shot a large seal this evening. It will net us about 125 pounds of meat.

A lane next to our floe is about three-quarters of a mile wide and extends south two miles. Its northern limit cannot be seen. Our floe is slowly settling back to the west and south, toward its former position, at the same time revolving in the opposite direction to the movement of the sun.

Hereafter, we are not to know the result of Israel's observations. Lieut. Greely thinks that the men will become discouraged and has given Israel orders that our actual position is to be told only to himself.

September 17th.

Our floe spun around last night and now faces just the opposite direction from yesterday. Instead of looking north we look in the direction of Cocked Hat Island. Strange to say, Nature has at last been kind. The change brings us a little nearer our goal.

Minimum temperature last night 2.5°.

Fred shot another seal this morning.

We started south with our sledges at 1 p.m. I went ahead as usual. On the whole, travelling was fairly good. We found two excellent floes over which we made splendid time.

Turned in at 11 p.m. After ten hours of the severest physical strain, to lie down in our sleeping bags and stretch our weary limbs, was indeed refreshing. As the bags were spread on the ice with only one thickness of canvas underneath them, our comfort can well be imagined. Even so, this has been the brightest day since leaving Fort Conger. At least, we have not drifted further into the unknown.

September 18th.

We turned out of our bags at an early hour with the intention of making a desperate effort to reach the land which now appears not far off. We drifted slightly to the south and east during the night. The minimum temperature was 9°.

For about half an hour we travelled over a smooth floe making good time. Finding a lane of water, we returned and brought up the remainder of our stores. The boat was then launched and our effects ferried from one floe to another. The ice was broken and moving about rapidly and it is yet a matter of great surprise how we ever escaped being separated in that grinding mass.

During the entire day, from 8 a.m. to 6 p.m., we worked in this manner, expecting every moment that the day's labor would terminate with fatal results. While crossing one dangerous place, Rice missed his footing and tumbled head foremost into the water.

At 6:30 p.m. we had reached a large circular floe. about a mile in diameter. We halted to rest and the cooks prepared supper. I was sent ahead by Lieut. Greely and on my return reported a lane on the opposite side. It evidently extended to the land, probably not more than three miles away, but no flag, cairn or other signal was visible from where I stood although I examined the coast carefully with the marine glasses.

We crossed the floe to the water's edge with the last load at 9 p.m., making thirteen hours of hard labor. We bivouacked there, spreading our bags on the uneven surface for a few hours rest. We intend to make an early start in the morning.

September 19th.

Alas! we were again doomed to bitter disappointment. Misfortune and calamity, hand in hand, have clung to us along the entire line of this retreat and were we at all superstitious we could readily believe that our end is not far off. Our high hopes of escape once more have been dashed. We have been driven back into the midst of Kane Sea.

About midnight a southwest gale sprang up. We are further north and east than ever before, perhaps twenty miles from land. To cross the floes over this distance seems a hopeless undertaking when we can average only about a mile and a quarter per day. And now we have been shown what child's play the wind can make of our struggles. How can we put our heart and strength into hauling the sledges!

We retired last evening without having erected the tepee and this morning our bags were filled with drift, and dripping with spray from the huge waves which broke against the southern edge of the floe. As nothing could be done we spent the day in our sleeping bags, listening to the roar of the waves and meditating over our helplessness.

To our intense relief the gale abated at 6 p.m.

Lieut. Greely at once called a council. The general wish was to remain here until the floe gets settled. Lieut. Greely favors an attempt to reach the Greenland coast by abandoning everything except twenty days provisions, records, boat and sledge. Madness!

September 20th.

Cloudy, foggy and fresh northerly winds, a low temperature; nothing but water and debris ice in sight, and a severe snow-storm this evening. Could anything be more wretched than having all these troubles at once? We are now carrying burdens of woe sufficient to crush ordinary men, but our party is of the right sort.

Our drift is tending toward Greenland. Only occasional glimpses of the coast can be obtained. Fred shot a large bladder nose seal this afternoon.

English stearine is now used for cooking. Alcohol is far superior and much more economical.

September 21st.

A heavy snowfall during the night. A northwest gale did not materially alter our position. We have been confined closely to our sleeping bags all day because of the weather. The bags are soaking wet from the effects of drifting snow which melts almost as soon as it falls.

Jens shot three small seals today.

Rice and those belonging to the boat crew built an ice-house to shelter them from the raging storms.

Connell and Ralston are quite ill with the flux.

Schneider has been adding canvas tops to our leather boots to help out our scanty supply of foot-gear. The ration of hard bread has been reduced from sixteen ounces to ten ounces per day.

September 22nd.

The sun appeared for a short time this morning.

At an early hour Bender reported seeing the mast with flag waving of one of our abandoned boats about two miles west of our position. Lieut. Greely at once ordered a party in which I was included, to put off in the ice-boat and attempt to reach it. We crossed a lane about half a mile wide and, leaving the boat Rice, Jens and I went across the floe in the direction of the abandoned boat. It proved to be the whale-boat which we thought in Baffin Bay ere this. We had reached within a few hundred yards of it when we were stopped by a lane filled with sludge ice and could not reach the boat.

Judging from occasional glimpses of the land, our position has not materially changed during the last three days. Israel's bearings place us about fourteen miles east of Cape Sabine.

We have transferred the tepee to a snow-bank for greater comfort. The snow is not so cold as the ice and will not melt as quickly. Last night a large pool formed under Cross's bag and his clothing was drenched. Resting was so disagreeable, in fact, that the natives got up and went out hunting long before day to avoid the misery.

SUNDAY, *September 23rd.*

Cold, stormy day with a high southeast wind. We appear to be drifting slowly back to our old position near Cocked Hat Island. Judging from the direction in which our floe is drifting, there must be a current to the west through Hayes Sound.

Dr. Pavy has a large corps of patients, all down with the flux.

We now eat seal blubber without any feeling of repugnance.

Lieut. Greely has directed me to go out tomorrow on the chance of obtaining a foot-hold on the whale-boat floe.

September 24th.

I went out this morning according to instructions. Leaving a party to watch the boat, Lieut. Lockwood and I with Jens proceeded toward the floe on which we could see the whale-boat. We had not gone far before we heard Bender calling to us, and his frantic gestures warned us that something serious had happened. We hurried back. And none too soon. A narrow crack which we had crossed was rapidly widening. The ice bent, crumbled and broke beneath our feet with that dismal groaning sound which will appall even the stoutest heart. We quickly took a running jump over the lane and landed on the opposite side in safety.

Game is getting scarce. Only one seal was seen today.

September 25th.

This floe is worse than a prison. The pack is in motion everywhere—grinding, crumbling and piling

ice high about the edges. At one time this morning
the pressure was so great that the small corner on
which we are camped broke away, the crack running
quite near our tepee. We drifted apart from the
larger portion of the floe before we could transfer to
it. The thick atmosphere soon placed it out of sight
and we are now stranded on a small block of ice with
which the wind, tides and currents easily can have
their way. To add to our misery of mind, the wind
changed at 2 p.m. to northeast and shortly afterward
increased to a gale, driving us down past Cape Sabine
where we had hoped eventually to land because of
the cache supposed to be there.

For the last few days we have had no watch or
guard during the night, but with the many dangers
which surround us, one was set tonight.

September 26th.

I can never forget our experiences since yesterday.
The suspense of the last few hours has been a terrible
strain. A wild and awful night was passed in the
driving storm with the dark water foaming about us
and we momentarily were expecting to be swallowed
by the waves. Our crippled floe has again broken,

scarcely leaving us space on which to stand with our boats and stores.

We cannot stay here long. This piece of ice will not survive much rough handling. But where can we step off? The violence of the storm has formed a large pool between us and land, and the waves unhampered by ice, come rolling against our raft, throwing spray over those who have the temerity to approach near the edge. We have been driven down past Payer Harbor and Rosse Bay at an alarming speed.

The cooks were called long before daylight to prepare breakfast, that we might be ready at the first streak of dawn to take advantage of the open water and reach the coast. But when daylight revealed the land, it was full six miles away and one-third of that distance the water was covered with debris ice through which no boat could be forced. The remainder was a seething, foaming ocean which would have swamped us in a moment.

At 7 a.m. we were in latitude 78° 37′. Owing to the heavy pack east of us, we are being driven directly south rather than southwest, as the direction of the wind would tend to carry us. Should we be

driven into Baffin Bay, as everything at present indi-
cates, we are inevitably lost.   .

Shortly after seven o'clock when the storm was at
its height we had another setback.   Our small floe
began to crumble and we were forced to move east-
ward to another of the pack.   The storm was driving
fine particles of snow in our faces and we were barely
able to make the necessary effort to escape.   The
snow-house which Rice and his party had constructed
was crushed by an overlapping floe.

Fully one-third our number are badly ill with the
flux.   This is attributed to the excessive use of salt
water and also to the fresh seal meat.

September 27th.

The weather continues wretched in the extreme.
The atmosphere is so thick that we cannot see the
coast and consequently do not know where we are,
or whether or not we are yet drifting.   Rice and his
party have no shelter for their sleeping bags and
their condition is miserable.   They were so wretched,
in fact, that they refused to come out of their bags
for a drink of rum for supper.   No breakfast could
be cooked because of the drifting snow.

Our bags are filled with drift, our clothing wet and everyone feels that there is little pleasure in life after all.

New victims of the flux continue to appear. I am one of them.

September 28th.

The gale has subsided somewhat. Toward evening I went out accompanied by Eskimo Fred to see if anything could be done to escape. We found a lane of water about half a mile wide. It offered excellent advantages.

We have remained in this position since yesterday—at the entrance to Baird Inlet near the northern shore. Our floe has lodged against a grounded iceberg. Had it not been for this act of Providence, we would have been driven into Baffin Bay.

As no movement appeared in the ice while I was watching, I returned to camp and reported the favorable opportunity. The sledge was hastily loaded and hauled to the lane where the boat was launched. Lieut. Greely placed Rice in charge of the boat to ferry our supplies and the party across. While he was transferring the first load, the remainder of the party went back after the other stores. Everything was taken across in seven loads and landed on an excellent floe about a mile broad.

At the extremity of this floe we were stopped by new ice and had to go into camp for the night. We made about two miles and are now perhaps one mile from land with good prospects of landing in the morning. An ill wind can upset these prospects.

September 29th.

Shore at last! On land once more!

Early this morning when the cooks were called, I was directed by Lieut. Greely to advance toward the land and select a route for the sledges. We had been deceived last evening into supposing land only one mile distant. In reality it was over four miles.

The conditions of travelling were highly favorable to our sledges and the start was made almost immediately after my return (7 a.m.). We ferried over two narrow lanes before gaining the shore. This was tiresome work with our several loads and dangerous, too, for it meant separating the party and abandoning some while the transfer from floe to floe was carried out.

The last load reached the coast at 6 p.m. The entire party was much exhausted by the work. We are camped among barren, snow-covered rocks at the base of a high, conical-shaped hill. In the midst of Kane Sea this hill frequently was a conspicuous landmark and guide. The Commanding Officer fixes our position as directly south of Leffert Glacier. We are many miles south of Cape Sabine, our actual destination.

Although the natives hunted all day they have killed nothing. Several ravens and a brace of ducks were observed flying about us during the march. The former are birds of ill-omen and many remarks were heard from the superstitious.

Cross, I am sorry to say, again has abused the confidence reposed in him. As he could not work in the drag ropes on account of his bad foot, he was left with the first load while the party went back for the second. On returning they found him intoxicated.

SUNDAY, *September 30th.*

Lieut. Greely directed Corporal Salor and Frederik to reconnoiter in the direction of Wade Point (south) to examine the condition of the ice for travelling with sledges, and also to see if there are provisions at the south cape of Rosse Bay. They returned in a few hours and Salor reported that lanes of water alternating with young ice had prevented their reaching land.

On learning that the route was impracticable, Rice at once volunteered to go with Jens north to Cape Sabine and learn whether a relief vessel had landed a cache of provisions there. He was granted permission to make this hazardous journey and will start tomorrow taking rations for four days.

As far as I can see, it is more than probable we will be compelled to pass the winter in this locality. With our miserable little boat and the channel choked with ice, there is not the slightest possibility of crossing to Littleton Island for information of the cache which should be there.

Near our landing place, Whisler discovered three ancient Eskimo huts and I found heaps of stones under which the natives formerly left caches of meat. Lieut. Greely has named the spot Eskimo Point.

Game is scarce—very. The natives killed nothing today. We are deluding ourselves in believing relief will yet come this fall.

October 1st.

Weather cloudy. The sun has sunk so low in the heavens that Israel could not get an observation and the stars are obscured by clouds.

Rice and Jens started at 8:30 a.m.

Long killed a walrus today, but before the kayak could reach him he disappeared beneath the water.

October 2nd.

I took an inventory of the commissary stores last evening and found only 35 days full rations of bread and meat remained. These rations can be extended to 50 days, if we subject ourselves to a greatly reduced diet, but the suffering will be extreme in this low temperature where a man requires from two to three times the normal diet. Also, we have some very hard labor ahead of us incident to the building of winter quarters.

Fifty more days will bring us to November 15th and, at that time, we should be either on the Greenland side or else in Baffin Bay. Lieut. Greely insists that when only ten days provisions remain he will attempt to across the sound to Littleton Island no matter what the consequences.

Lieut. Greely directed Lieut. Lockwood and me to select a building site for the winter quarters. We found an excellent place well-sheltered by the mountain on one side and the glacier on the other two.

Long and Eskimo Fred have been detailed as permanent hunters. They killed nothing today. The native says that the game has all left the pool about the grounded bergs in our vicinity and taken refuge in open water.

Hard bread was reduced to six ounces; potatoes to one and one-half, and meat to twelve ounces. One ounce of extract of beef was added to the ration.

October 3rd.

We began building our three winter huts this morning. Three ancient Eskimo igloos furnished abundant building material and when we had ceased work this evening the stone foundations were well advanced. Light snow fell and a high wind made the day very disagreeable.

The hunters saw a few walruses but no seals. A solitary snow bunting evidently lost from its mate hopped about camp in search of crumbs and chirped mournfully.

October 4th.

Clear, beautiful weather. This is a great advantage to poor Rice and Jens while on their journey to Cape Sabine. A gale from the N.E. last night threatened to relieve us of our shelter—the tepee. The temperature is falling slowly.

Our houses are progressing. At 2 p.m. we knocked off work and hauled down a load of stores left at our old camp.

The roaring and grinding noise coming from the pack in the channel is frightful to hear. There is not the slightest sign of water.

October 5th.

The day was foggy and disagreeable.

The walls of my house were completed and the interior filled with moss. It was decided to use the boat as a roof for one of the buildings. Lots were drawn and my mess has won the prize.

No game today except a ptarmigan shot by Cross.

October 6th.

Lieut. Greely detailed a "board" to make a division of the oars and other material for the building of our huts. He had appointed me as one of the commission, but I requested to be excused. As I have charge of one mess, I felt that I might be accused of unfairness in my recommendations. Notwithstanding my precautions, Israel did accuse me of being the leader in a "grab game," as he expressed it, and looking out too well for my own party. I took him before the Commanding Officer where he repeated his charges. Lieut. Greely exonerated me from all blame, but that has not left some of my comrades altogether certain of my honesty. All the trouble was really caused by the fault-finding of Connell.

The houses were covered today and we moved in. Long and Fred each shot a seal. Only one was secured.

SUNDAY, *October 7th.*

A clear beautiful day. The Greenland coast rose up before us prominently, every irregularity in the land being distinctly outlined. How we all wish we could reach that land with its promise of abundant game and safety!

Although this is the Sabbath, construction work continued all day.

Rice is now due. We have been watching eagerly for him, not only to learn what he found but to know that he has come through the trip safely. Ellis and Whisler were sent over the glacier to meet him, but dense fog turned them back.

Connell has been charged with misconduct and reduced from sergeant to the grade of private. Linn was advanced to sergeant.

I learned this evening that a feeling of dissatisfaction existed because it was believed I showed partiality in issuing hard bread to "a favorite few." I immediately asked Lieut. Greely to relieve me from the duties of 1st Sergeant and detail some one else to issue provisions. He said that he had implicit confidence in me and refused to relieve me from this thankless duty. It is certainly hard to endure these reflections on my fairness, especially when I have tried so hard to satisfy all.

Long and Fred shot a walrus on the floe, but the creature had life enough to roll into the water and escape, leaving the ice and the pool where he sank stained with his blood.

Israel came to me this morning and apologized for his unjust accusations of last evening. He said he had been influenced by others to make the remarks.

October 8th.

Rice has not yet returned. He is probably detained by new ice or a storm. God grant that he comes back to us in safety. We cannot spare such a noble soul from our party.

Bender made me a pair of scales which, though crude, will greatly assist in weighing out the scanty allowance of food. A mischievous fox visited the camp last night and succeeded in stealing three-quarters of a pound of meat.

Frederik shot two seals, but both sank before he could squeeze himself into his kayak and secure them. It is heart-rending to see this food which is our very life disappear before our eyes.

October 9th.

Rice returned at 4 p.m. having found records at Cape Sabine and vicinity which place us in possession of unwelcome and disheartening facts. The first record stated that in the summer of 1882 the steam sealer *Neptune* of St. John's, N.F., under Capt. Sopp had visited Smith Sound and endeavored to reach Lady Franklin Bay, but was turned back by the pack near Victoria Head. The expeditionary force was commanded by Major Beebe who is a member of the Signal Corps, but Lieut. Greely remembers him as the private secretary to General Hazen. All the stores of this vessel were to be taken back, judging from the record which is not altogether clear. Two hundred and forty rations were landed just west of Cape Sabine and a duplicate depot established at Littleton Island.

The second record was signed by Lieut. E. A. Garlington, 7th Cavalry, U.S.A., and stated that the *Proteus* which was coming to our relief this year was crushed by the ice in Smith Sound on July 23rd, and everything except a few provisions and a quantity of clothing lost. His own party of fourteen with Capt. Pike and twenty-one men were going to cross to Littleton Island and endeavor to communicate with a steamer. The record states that the U.S.S. *Yantic* has orders to come as far north as Littleton Island and that "a Swedish vessel will reach Cape York sometime this month" (July). This record states there is a whale-boat cached on this shore to the south at Cape Isabella. Whether it was left by the Beebe expedition, the *Yantic* or Lieut. Garlington, the record does not say. Since a boat was landed there, some of our party are inclined to think there must be supplies at Cape Isabella as well. The boat, of course, was cached in accordance with the retreat plan laid out by Lieut. Greely in a letter sent to General Hazen before the *Proteus* left us at Fort Conger. If we are able to cross the sound, it will be useful.

The finding of these records has dissipated all the day dreams of rescue which we have been fostering, and brought us face to face with our situation as it really is. It could hardly be much worse. There are little more than 1,000 rations at Cape Sabine and these will not go far toward feeding twenty-five men. [A ration is one day's food for one man. The rations found at Cape Sabine normally would have fed the Greely party for forty days.] Little time remains to hunt and besides game has grown noticeably scarce.

Lieut. Greely, after a consultation, has decided to abandon these huts and move the party to Cape Sabine. It would be a difficult task to bring the rations here. Anyway, we assume from Lieut. Garlington's record, that he will try to return to Cape Sabine, for he wrote that "everything within the power of

man to rescue" would be done for our party. We
will take the first load to Rosse Bay tomorrow, the
party returning the same day to this camp.

Rice found that Rosse Bay and Buchanan Strait
were connected by a narrow strait. This makes Cape
Sabine an island. The new discovery received the
name of Rice Strait in honor of the man through
whose heroism and devotion it was found.

[So much for the fashion in which Greely and his
men received the news of the fate of the two efforts
made to reach them with relief. So much for the situation this news left them in: thrown upon their own
resources one thousand miles north of the Arctic circle, on a blizzard-swept sheet of rock and ice as barren
as the moon, inadequately mapped, and scarcely
known to ship, man, bird or beast, without shelter,
without fuel and with forty-odd days' rations to face
the northern winter night which in a few days would
be upon them. The sole ray of hope was that Garlington or the *Yantic* people had established a party to
winter on Littleton Island, as called for by orders.
This hope sustained Greely and his men in their extremity. Littleton Island was just across Smith
Sound from Cape Sabine, only twenty-three miles

distant. From now on neither the eyes nor the thoughts of the men are long away from that small stretch of water separating them from this Promised Land of food and warmth. When the sea was free of ice, they thought surely rescuers would arrive by boat. When the sea was covered with ice, they speculated on relief coming by sledge. And when relief did not come by boat or sledge the starving party made their own attempts to get word across the Sound. A few of the Greely band were to live long enough to learn the whole truth. There was no relief party on Littleton Island. That hope like every other hope thus far cherished proved to be a delusion. The history of the relief efforts of 1882 and 1883 remains, therefore, a flawless record of misfortune and blundering.]

October 10th.

A heavy snow-storm prevented us from going to Rosse Bay. The sledge, however, was loaded and we will start at the first opportunity.

Rice again has volunteered for a hazardous duty— to go south to Cape Isabella and learn if any provisions were left with the whale-boat. While there he will try to find the English cache of 144 pounds of preserved meat left by Captain Nares in 1875.

The temperature has been very high during this storm. A few ravens were observed today flying over our huts and uttering ominous croaks.

October 11th.

The sky was bright and clear today and the spirits of our party naturally rose. Minimum recorded temperature last night 7°.

Rice and Fred left for Cape Isabella at an early hour. The sledge party started at 6:45 a.m. for Rosse Bay and returned at 3:15 p.m. Cross again was found in a beastly state of intoxication after we had left him with one load while we advanced the other. I reported the circumstance to Lieut. Greely, but nothing can be done now. Violent measures could be resorted to, but no one wishes to bring disgrace to the expedition at this late date.

Tomorrow we abandon these huts and take up the march for Cape Sabine. Long shot a forty pound seal this evening.

October 12th.

Minimum temperature −8.5°.

Canvas, ropes, oars and poles from which we constructed the hut roofs were all taken with us. The ice-boat *Beaumont* was left on the skeleton walls of my hut. We started with two sledges at 8 a.m., with all property and provisions on them. After seven hours of exhausting labor, we reached Rosse Bay and halted for camp.

The small sledge will not be used by this party again. The roughly shod runners cause great friction. Hereafter double trips will be made with the large sledge.

This is a cold, disagreeable evening. My fingers are so nearly frozen that I can scarcely clasp my pencil. Of course, we feel the cold and strain of our labors more than ordinarily because of our reduced diet.

Despite the raw, chilling winds, our bags were spread on the ice-covered rocks and without shelter or any protection we have prepared to pass a wretched night. A small issue of rum.

October 13th.

A long, long night. Unprotected from the cold, we were unable to sleep in our frozen bags.

Crossing Rosse Bay we kept close to the face of the glacier. The ice in many places was thin and treacherous, but it was necessary to rely on chance and so we travelled over spots which would bend and crack beneath our weight. If we were not so thoroughly disheartened by the turn of events, we might be more cautious.

Camp was made at the entrance to Rice Strait and the two loads deposited there after nine hours work. Hauling was comparatively easy, but when bringing in the second load we had a scare which took our breath away. A terrible crash was suddenly heard and just in front of us the ice was torn asunder as with an invisible hand. A huge block of ice, detached from the base of the berg close by, shot up, protruding many feet in the air and throwing fragments of ice in every direction. For a moment I felt as if some mighty leviathan of the deep was aiming at our destruction. At any rate, occasional incidents of this kind are a variation from the depressing monotony of our marches.

Made good about six miles. The total distance travelled, however, was eighteen miles. High wind. Alcohol allowance not sufficient to cook supper.

SUNDAY, *October 14th.*

High wind accompanied by snow.

After breakfasting on dog pemmican (raw), we broke camp at 8:15 a.m. Rice Strait was not entirely frozen in the middle and we had to hug the shore closely. The sledge threatened to break through many places, but fortune favored us. Had the sledge gone, we would have lost our stores.

The two trips were made in about nine hours and the distance made good six miles. A fine hot supper this evening caused us to forget all our woes. The last drop of rum was issued.

Henry has frosted one of his feet slightly. Our shoes and clothing are far from adequate. Henry, by the way, was observed eating some of the raw seal intestines with evident relish.

We have camped on the rocks without shelter of any kind, except our sleeping bags.

October 15th.

We passed the worst night of our lives in a howling storm. One thickness of hide, frozen as hard as flint, could not keep out cold. Temperature –1°.

Lieut. Greely, Gardiner and Jens started in advance of the party to select a route through the hummocks. Main party left camp at 7:30 a.m. and travelled along the coast past Cocked Hat Island toward Cape Sabine. In order to proceed more quickly we left a large cache of stores which we will not require for our immediate use. The sledge broke and, leaving another portion of our load on the floe, we advanced with the remainder reaching the wreck cache of the *Proteus* about three miles from Cape Sabine at 2:30 p.m.

We eagerly overhauled the cache, but were much disappointed to find so little. Of vegetables, raisins, lemons, clothing, boxes, looking-glasses, etc., there was a profuse display. Also about twenty pounds of Durham tobacco and ten of plug. A portion of this was issued to the smokers, the others receiving a quantity of raisins instead.

Rice and Frederik arrived from Cape Isabella soon after we had camped. They report having found 144 pounds of canned meat at Isabella which had been deposited by Capt. Nares [the English explorer who visited that point in 1875], but they were unable to locate the boat which the Garlington record said was there.

October 16th.

A large party was dispatched under Lockwood to bring up the stores abandoned on the floe when the sledge broke yesterday. Lieut. Greely, Rice and myself went to the Beebe cache to prepare it for transportation to this camp. Lieut. Kislingbury and Jens went to Payer Harbor to examine the clothing cache. We brought the wall tent from the cache and Rice and I afterward returned to get a quantity of Medford rum.

The party under Lieut. Lockwood returned at about 2:30 p.m., and all hands were at once turned out to build the walls of a snow-house of blocks cut from a neighboring drift. The top was covered with the oars and spare sails. It was a poor shelter but better than any we have had since leaving Eskimo Point.

October 17th.   •

A strong northwest wind blew during the night, sifting the snow through the crevices of our hut and rendering the already pitiable condition of our party ten times worse than before. With our large party and the few rations at our disposal, our prospects are dark.

The Beebe cache has been moved up to camp. Our whale-boat was also brought up. It is badly broken and we have nothing with which to repair it.

October 18th.

Cold—very cold—and the disagreeable snow continues to fall.

Lieut. Greely consulted with the party about the site for our permanent winter quarters. A neck of land about halfway between Cape Sabine and Cocked Hat Island was chosen because of the fresh water lake nearby. It is fed by a glacier of the island. The site is about half a mile from our first camp and so all our provisions will have to be transferred.

The walls of our quarters already have been started. The hut in which our twenty-five are to live, possibly all winter, will be twenty-five feet long and eighteen feet wide, the walls about four feet high. The party to a man is working well and the building already is nearly completed.

Frederik shot a blue fox this evening.

October 19th.

Cloudy weather and a fresh southwest wind with

temperature at −9°. These climatic conditions are not conducive to our comfort and happiness. Comfort, in fact, is something of the past.

The whale-boat has been placed lengthwise on the frame of the hut and the oars nailed into place as rafters. Over this framework we stretched canvas and then thinly coated it with snow.

In the low temperature it was a day of exhausting labor for everyone and we were all in our sleeping bags at 5 p.m.

II

STARVATION

October 20th.

Temperature −13°.

The roof of our dwelling was completed this morning and snow blocks were prepared for the construction of a wall about the hut. We have placed a small quantity of gravel on the floor to keep our sleeping bags from the snow and ice.

Our winter's schedule of provisions was discussed this evening. It is far from an attractive one to hungry men. With strict limitations, we can extend our food until March 10, 1884, at which time we hope to be either with a relief expedition or with Eskimo natives at Littleton Island. If not, what then?

Sunday, *October 21st.*

A party under Lieut. Lockwood went to Rice Strait and hauled in the load we left there several days ago. Long volunteered to hunt with the two natives and so they were left in camp there with the wall tent. We returned with the load, exhausted from our efforts. Everyone complains of excessive weakness and some stagger while walking.

A lemon was issued to each of us this morning in lieu of lime-juice. The scraps of newspapers in which the lemons were wrapped have been removed and carefully dried for future reading. It will be a rare treat to receive news again from the civilized world. We have already learned from scraps that Garfield died and Arthur is President.

October 22nd.

Rice with three men was ordered to Cape Sabine to bring up a few articles of clothing. He was also directed to place in the cairn on Brevoort Island a record which Lieut. Greely had prepared telling of our deplorable condition. This was done to guide to us any party from Littleton Island reaching these shores.

Ellis celebrates his forty-third birthday.

October 23rd.

Temperature —16°.

We took pendulum and records to Payer Harbor
and cached them with the English depot of provisions. As we were returning with a portion of this
depot, our sledge broke down and we came home
without it. This made a very bad impression on some
of the men who are exceedingly discouraged.

October 24th.

Snow falling heavily and a high northwest wind
makes a considerable drift.

Twelve of us again went down to Payer Harbor
to haul in the sledge. Elison made repairs, but soon
after starting it broke again and was abandoned
until tomorrow. The men again were very tired and
weak from the prolonged exertion and the effects of
the meagre diet.

October 26th.

Party again started from Cape Sabine at 7 a.m.
The sledge broke down under the heavy load and
unable to continue the struggle we at once abandoned
it and returned to the house.

There is a vast space of open water to the north but
very little toward the Greenland coast. The hunt-

ers were out all day, but returned without game.

The sun disappeared below the horizon today to reappear no more until the latter part of February. I wonder how many of us will ever look on its face again!

October 27th.

The weather is cloudy and disagreeable. The lowest temperature yet experienced here was recorded last night, −22°.

The sledge was once more repaired and this time the party which went out for the abandoned load was able to get it into camp. I personally have never participated in a more disagreeable task. The combination of hunger, cold and scant clothing easily took the heart out of our work.

The commissary was broken into last night and a small quantity of hard bread taken. While one can sympathize with the hunger which drives a member of our party to commit such a despicable act, still the culprit will have to be brought to light and punished.

Lieut. Greely has named this place Camp Clay in honor of the Mr. Clay who was to have been a member of the expedition, but left it [in Greenland] when he and Dr. Pavy could no longer remain friends. According to an article written in May 1883 and salvaged from the lemons, Mr. Clay has been making noble efforts in behalf of our rescue.

SUNDAY, *October 28th.*

We started for Cape Sabine this morning for another load of clothing. On the return trip, the sledge again broke. Such failures are discouraging and we have spent the day moodily contemplating our dismal future in this land.

What are we to do? As far as I can see, there is nothing ahead of us except starvation. Every hope of rescue this fall has failed us. How can we hope for anything now from a relief expedition? The civilized world has forgotten us in our hour of need. While those on whom we have depended for rescue are surrounded by comforts and luxuries, this shivering band of wretched creatures must fight starvation and the frost of an Arctic winter. And for what? We have food until March 10th. There is nothing to look forward to after that.

The hunters could not go out today on account of a storm.

October 29th.

I issued clothing today. The garments are covered with ice and have to be thawed and dried by the heat from the body.

The sledge was again repaired and another load hauled from Payer Harbor. Everyone of the sledgers were exhausted after the trip. The strongest members of the party seem to break down first. Our weakness from hunger is increasing visibly. We will be able to undertake few more hauling trips.

The barometer was placed in position so that regular observations will now be taken at this point.

The rations again have been reduced slightly, but those detailed for sledging will receive two ounces extra each morning.

To prevent our minds from becoming torpid, an hour or so each evening is devoted to reading aloud. Gardiner reads the Bible, Lieut. Greely, the army regulations (a copy was left for this abandoned Polar party in the wreck cache!) and Rice, one of Hardy's novels. "Two in a Tower."

October 30th.

The hunters—Long, Eskimo Fred and Jens—

went to Rice Strait this morning taking provisions for three days.

Thirteen of us again went to Cape Sabine for a load of provisions.

Rice has volunteered to lead a party to Cape Isabella to secure the 144 pounds of meat, cached by the English. He will be accompanied by three others. Elison is trying to manufacture them a sledge of the scanty material we can supply.

Bender killed a fox this morning. The little animal had his head in a small tin can and so his capture was easy.

An approximate estimate of the provisions placed the limit at March 10th, if our allowance is kept at fifteen ounces each per day. In this cold climate can we live long on such a small ration? At Fort Conger the daily ration was seventy ounces per man.

October 31st.

Thank God! The last load of supplies was brought from Cape Sabine this evening.

The whale-boat which we abandoned last September in the pack, drifted down on the large floe on which we had left it, and fortunately for us lodged between Brevoort Island and Cape Sabine. It has been broken up for fuel. We could not use the boat now in the attempt to cross the channel.

Cloud-berries, the Swedish anti-scorbutic, were issued the messes this evening.

November 1st.

Lieut. Kislingbury is very ill from the effects of yesterday's exertion. The Doctor thinks the strain will result in rupture. While undergoing an examination this evening he fainted twice. Poor fellow! He is entirely dependent on his companions for assistance. Lieut. Lockwood and Dr. Pavy have loaned him the mattress which fell to them by lot.

Elison has cut down the six-man sledge to a four-man sledge for Rice's contemplated journey to Cape Isabella. Fredericks, Linn and Elison have been detailed to accompany Rice. They are all brave fellows and the entire party feels that if there is a chance of bringing the meat to Camp Clay they will do it. God grant that they all will come through safely. I have issued them provisions for eight days.

Schneider was lucky enough to shoot a white fox

which he detected prowling about our scanty stores.

Bender has manufactured a small sheet-iron stove on which our cooking will be done in future. The barrels and boxes left in the Garlington caches, oars, boats, etc. will be used for fuel.

The party now is divided into two messes. The rations, except bread and meat which are given out daily, are issued every Wednesday. Each mess alternates in the order of cooking, one cooking first one day and the other the next.

From this date, Lieut. Greely has reduced our provisions per man per day to the following:

	Ounces
Meat	4.
Extract of beef	0.26
Evaporated potatoes	0.4
Soup	0.6
Tomatoes	0.3
Peas	0.2
Corn	0.2
Carrots	0.1
Bread	6.
Dog-biscuit	0.8
Butter	0.5

Lard 0.26

Rice 0.1

Raisins 0.16

Tea 0.3

Extract of coffee 0.44

Extract of chocolate 0.3

Pickled onions 0.4

Milk 0.2

This makes little more than fourteen ounces of food a day on which we hope to sustain life. Dr. Pavy has refused to give his medical sanction to such a scanty diet. He says we cannot live long on it in this cold climate. The Commanding Officer believes that we have no chance for life at all unless we extend our supplies to the farthest possible limit. It is altogether probable no rescue party will be able to reach these shores until the ice begins to break in the sound next spring. Our chances of crossing to Littleton Island are remote, although Lieut. Greely speaks as though such an attempt will be made.

November 2nd.

Rice, Linn, Elison and Fredericks started for Cape Isabella at 8 a.m. What an ordeal they have

before them! They have been fed extra food for
several days, but even so their strength is far below
what it should be for this long trip in below zero
weather. They are equipped the best we could offer,
for every member of the party has denied himself
some article of clothing which will add to their
warmth and comfort.

Near our old camp I shot a blue fox which weighed
three and a half pounds. Ralston killed a white fox,
four and a half pounds.

The cooks prepared our evening meal over the
small stoves made by Bender. They work quite
satisfactorily. The amount of fuel consumed was
small and the stews boiled in only forty-eight
minutes. If we practice economy, the barrels should
last over eighty days.

November 3rd.

Long returned at 8 a.m. for a new supply of provisions with which to continue his hunting operations
at Rice Strait. He has killed only one seal weighing
about seventy-five pounds. The noble fellow is certainly persistent in his efforts to secure game for our
hungry party, notwithstanding the low temperature

and his weak condition. For shelter he and the natives have only a canvas tent and Long reports the temperature colder than at Camp Clay. Of course, they have no fire.

SUNDAY, *November 4th.*

A huge hard bread pudding for breakfast made us all feel very happy for a few hours. Sunday, the Commanding Officer has decreed, is always to be a feast day with some rare delicacy to look forward to. We also have an excellent stew made from fox carcasses.

The sense of repletion to the stomach after eating belongs to our pleasures of the past. The constant gnawing of hunger almost drives us mad. I wonder if we will retain control of our minds throughout the trying period which seems inevitable.

Long started back to Rice Strait at 8 a.m., taking with him provisions for five more days. At the end of that time we are to go down with the large sledge and haul up the tent, sleeping bag and the seal which he shot. We hope we will have to haul up more game than that, particularly since Long saw the tracks of two bears yesterday while returning to Camp Clay. A good-sized bear is just what this party needs to cheer it up.

The hut is imperfectly ventilated and the dense smoke from the cooking lamps gave us all a headache this morning. Something will have to be done to change this condition.

Although this is the Sabbath, we began work on the new commissary storehouse. Someone again has been purloining provisions from the storehouse. It is well we are preparing to lock up what food remains.

November 5th.

Although it is twenty degrees below zero outside, the temperature in the hut ranges from 24° to 36°. This enables us to feel very comfortable (?) at all times. Our room is lighted during the day from the flame of a small blubber lamp which gives about half the light of an ordinary tallow candle.

Lieut. Kislingbury is recovering slowly. All members are showing signs of more and more weakness. It is slow starvation.

November 6th.

The wall about the house is not progressing as rapidly as I would wish, but the poor fellows are so weak that one cannot in reason expect severe labor of them.

I examined the mixed tea and sugar of the English cache and found dampness had greatly deteriorated it.

Our conversations are almost entirely of cooking and the good dishes that we used to enjoy.

No foxes have been seen for several days. Our dirty faces and disreputable clothing must have frightened them. No one ever thinks of wasting what energy he has in cleaning his person, or fussing with his ragged garments.

November 7th.

Frederik came in from Rice Strait this morning having been sent by Long who wants the sledge down tomorrow. He is withdrawing now because of the prevailing high winds which prevent game from coming out.

I issued the provisions for the coming week today. Also I made a very welcome discovery about one of

our supplies. When we first arrived here, I estimated the weight of the blubber at two hundred
pounds, but actually it exceeds this estimate by ninety
pounds.

November 8th.

Temperature −31.5°.

In spite of the severe weather, seven of us, Lieut.
Lockwood in command, started at 7 a.m. with the
large sledge for Rice Strait. We reached the tent
at 10:30. We were very disappointed to learn that
the hunters had killed only the one seal reported a
few days ago.

Reached Camp Clay at 3:15 p.m., well-nigh exhausted. An issue of hot rum on our return was
never more welcome.

Schneider was found in the storehouse under very
suspicious circumstances. He was openly accused
of stealing provisions, but stoutly protested his innocence. Since he was intoxicated, his guilt was
obvious. Great indignation in language exceedingly
emphatic was expressed by everyone. Schneider
was promptly relieved of his duties as cook and
Bender detailed in his place.

November 9th.

Matters are growing worse. Lieut. Lockwood discovered a can of milk in the commissary storehouse, carefully covered by a block of snow. An attempt had been made to open it, but the contents fortunately were intact. Marks and scratches made in the hurry of opening corresponded with the nicks in Schneider's knife. But the knife had been loaned to Henry and was in his possession!

We do not know whom to trust in this extremity.

November 10th.

At midnight those lying awake were startled to hear the crisp snow breaking under footsteps approaching our hut. In a moment Rice entered the room—Rice back from Cape Isabella—but for a long time he was too exhausted to speak. At last he was able to gasp out, "Elison is dying." And then after another long period of waiting while he gained more strength, he was able to give us the details.

His party had reached Cape Isabella on the evening of the third day, all in fair condition. On starting back with the load of meat, Elison became exhausted. For several days his hands and feet had

shown a tendency to freeze, but his comrades on each
occasion were able to thaw them out. Now, however, his whole body seemed to lose all power to
resist the cold and his hands, arms, legs and feet
quickly froze up stiff. The men carried and dragged
him nearly across Baird Inlet, making double trips,
first for him and then for the meat, weakening their
strength and exposing themselves to the merciless
cold. Fredericks even carried Elison on his back until he could bear the burden no longer. And all the
while the frozen man was crying out his pain.

Rice saw that this state of travel could not continue and thereupon decided he would have to
abandon the meat, if Elison's life was to be saved.
The load of meat was left in the snow with one of
the Springfield rifles standing upright to mark the
spot. Elison was placed on the sledge and taken to
our old camp at Eskimo Point. Here Linn and
Fredericks crawled into the sleeping bag with him,
one on either side, to thaw him out. Rice tried to
cook them a warm meal, but a gale was blowing and
he could not get the cooking lamp lighted.

Taking a piece of frozen meat for himself Rice,
after all day in the drag ropes, walked the seventeen

miles from Eskimo Point to Camp Clay for relief. It was a noble, courageous act.

Fred and I were immediately ordered out by the Commanding Officer to carry food and relief to Elison. The large sledge with seven or eight men was to follow us under command of Lieut. Lockwood. As I left the hut, Rice told me that Elison probably would be dead before succor could reach him.

Outside the darkness was intense and Fred and I floundered about among the hummocks, frequently falling down. For me the tenseness of the situation was relieved from time to time by the half-suppressed English oaths uttered by my dusky companion as he stumbled and fell. Of these he knew none until the Lady Franklin Bay Expedition took him north.

About noon we reached the camp and found Elison a little better than when Rice departed. Linn and Fredericks had done a good job in thawing him with the heat of their bodies, but had greatly weakened themselves and severely frozen their faces and extremities.

I had difficulty in making a fire for the wind continued to blow, but finally was able to cook them a meat stew. I made hot, delicious drinks which gave them new life and restored their sluggish circulation. All three men were frozen into the sleeping bag and so without strength to free them, I had to feed them as well.

Elison was a pitiable sight with his frozen face and limbs. He called to me repeatedly to kill him that the others might escape alive. I tried to cheer him with the assurance that we would all escape and return to our homes together, but he would shake his head sadly and say in a low, pleading voice, "Please kill me, will you?"

Poor Fredericks and Linn! The night with Elison must have been a nightmare. He was in agony all the time, particularly when he began to thaw. Also, unable to control himself, he urinated frequently. Fredericks told me that he thought his continuous cries of pain had affected Linn's mind at one time during the night. Linn began to speak incoherently and wanted to leave the sleeping bag. Fredericks was hard put to it in persuading him to stay. And there the three of them lay with no shelter and very, very hungry, wondering whether Rice had been able to make it back to Camp Clay.

With the assistance of Linn and Fredericks I had

intended to take Elison on the sledge to meet the relief party, but they told me that they could not do anything more. In fact, they were not certain that they even could stand on their legs. I made them all as comfortable as possible and with Fred turned back, a howling blast in our faces, to meet Lieut. Lockwood.

Just before leaving, I observed a fox walk deliberately to the bag where the three lay and attempt to enter. I struck at him with an ax, but missed my aim.

We nearly reached Rice Strait before our sight was gladdened by the approaching relief party. I took my place in the drag ropes and returned to the south side of the bay where we went into camp at 5:10 p.m. The gale has been terrific all day.

SUNDAY, *November 11th.*

We had little rest last night because of the cold and wind. The cook was called at 4:30 a.m. and at 6 o'clock I started forward alone to prepare breakfast for Elison, Linn and Fredericks while the party broke camp.

During my absence, the poor fellows once more

had been unable to sleep and were shivering with the cold when I arrived. I cannot understand how they have survived—hungry, half frozen, the storm beating down on them incessantly and Elison delirious with pain. Linn and Fredericks are brave fellows to have stuck it out.

They were still frozen in the bag. I could do nothing for their release and started to prepare breakfast. The alcohol lamp would not burn and I next tried a few pieces of the ice-boat which they had brought from Eskimo Point. With this I was more successful, but at the expense of my poor fingers which alternately were burned and frosted. At last I had them some hot meat stew and was able to make them comparatively happy.

When the sledge party arrived, we chopped open the sleeping bag and liberated the occupants. Elison was placed in a single dogskin bag and wrapped warmly in a large piece of canvas. Linn and Fredericks walked about for a short time to stretch their stiffened limbs and then started ahead to walk the seventeen miles intervening between them and the warmth (?) of Camp Clay. The sledge started at 9:30 a.m.

At 5 p.m. we had reached the northern entrance
to Rice Strait and here halted to cook some tea. The
wind had been blowing in our faces in passing up
Rice Strait and everyone was chilled and so be-
numbed that we could scarcely erect the tent. Elison was taken inside and under the influence of
hopeful words and good-natured chaff regained
something of his old cheerfulness.

At 8:10 p.m. we again started with our sledge toward Camp Clay. As we entered Buchanan Strait,
the wind died away and the moon rose and shed soft
light over the barren ice-fields, making the night one
of the most attractive that I have ever known. The
ice-bound coast with the chaotic masses of pulverized
bergs at its borders and the weird scene of desolation
spreading about us on every side, were never so apparent as now. A feeling of awe seemed to take
possession of the party and we moved forward slowly
and in silence with our half-conscious burden.

November 12th.

After plodding along wearily for hours we reached
Camp Clay at 2:10 a.m. A party came out and
helped us haul the sledge over the ice-foot. Such

rejoicing was never before heard in our wretched hut because of our quick return, and never did rough-bearded men express more sympathy or tenderness for a crippled comrade.

Of the condition of the sledgers, I can speak only for myself. I am probably one of the strongest, but at no time in my life have my physical powers been called on to sustain such a trial as last evening. Even my will wavered. [The sledge party was seventeen hours on the march, but Sergeant Brainard who made the journey from Rice Strait before their start, had been continuously on duty for more than twenty hours.]

Dr. Pavy considers that amputation of Elison's limbs is absolutely necessary, but fears that this will result fatally. He and Biederbick with a corps of willing assistants worked hours to alleviate his sufferings.

Linn and Fredericks arrived at 4 p.m. last night, badly broken down physically. Linn almost went out of his head again, eating handfuls of snow as he grew more exhausted. Fredericks, though, bolstered him up and was able to get him into camp without any serious effect from the snow.

Temperature −34.5°.

November 13th.

The weather has been clear and the moon shining brilliantly all day.

The relief party is recovering from the effects of the exposure and hardships of the last few days. Elison's condition is very critical. Rice, Linn and Fredericks, although lame and sore from frost-bites and weakened by their terrible experience generally, are recovering under a generous treatment.

Biederbick shot a white fox which weighed five and a half pounds.

November 14th.

Nothing accomplished today. All the energy, and very naturally too, has disappeared from our little band. The bread ration was reduced one half ounce (6 to 5½). I issued the provisions in bulk for the ensuing week.

Biederbick sits up with Elison all night and Dr. Pavy watches over him during the day. He is feeling somewhat better, but still no hope is entertained for his complete recovery.

November 15th.

A fresh westerly wind and a temperature of −38.2° caused us to seek the seclusion of the hut during the greater part of the day. We worked, however, for a short time this morning plastering the vestibule of the commissary storehouse with moistened snow hoping to make the walls firm enough to resist the gales.

Elison appears to be improving slowly.

Someone broke into the commissary last night. . . .

November 17th.

I have placed a wooden door with a lock in the commissary storehouse which, I hope, will be an effectual bar to all midnight intruders.

The patients are improving slowly notwithstanding the small amount of provisions on which we are now living. Our eyes and lungs are very much affected by the thick smoke which is unavoidable in cooking with this damp wood.

Lieut. Greely contributed to the morning's entertainment by lecturing on the physical geography of North America, confining himself more particularly to the United States. This is to be followed by lectures on astronomy by Israel, and on France, natural history and physiology by Dr. Pavy. All of us will contribute to the evening's entertainment by conversing on various subjects, particularly those relating to food, and in reading from the few books in our possession.

SUNDAY, *November 18th.*

Rice and myself placed a flag on one of our spare oars and planted it on the extreme outer point of this peninsula where it may readily be seen by a relief party.

November 19th.

Calm and cloudy. Temperature −35.2°.

I opened the remaining barrel of dog biscuits today and was agreeably surprised to find all except a few pieces in excellent condition. This is food which any well-bred dog would refuse, but if we had plenty of it, I for one would be happier. As it is the quantity which we now receive is only an aggravation to our appetites.

Long and Jens each shot a fox today. Instead of

being issued in lieu of our regular meat ration, this game is added to our Sunday evening meal. The intestines, in fact everything except the skin, are used for our stews and eaten without the slightest feeling of repugnance.

Some person who did not fear the just vengeance of an outraged party was heard fumbling about the hard bread can belonging to one of the messes. Before a light could be struck he decamped. Night before last a piece of English chocolate was stolen from Long, the cook in Lieut. Greely's mess. . . .

November 21st.

The routine of our life in this wretched hut is as follows: The cooks are called at 6 a.m. Breakfast is usually ready at 7 and eaten sitting up in our sleeping bags. This over and while the cooks are cleaning up, the conversation becomes general. Favored subjects are cookery and the good dishes which we remember to have partaken of in the past.

Between 9 and 11 Lieut. Greely discourses on the geography of the United States. I then go out and issue provisions to the cooks for the following day. One of the others goes to the lake to cut a hole through the ice and provide water for cooking. It is also this man's duty to empty the large urinal tub kept in the alley.

At 2:30 the cooks light their fire for dinner, and at about 4 o'clock the meal is served. We then sit up and converse on all sorts of subjects until 6 when the readings begin. We usually retire between eight and nine o'cock.

The list of invalids I record as follows: Lieut. Kislingbury, rupture, is now convalescent. Henry, toe frost-bitten, very bad. Elison, extremities frozen, lower limbs to knees, condition critical. Gardiner, felon on fore finger, improving slowly. Linn, rheumatism, and system broken down, from recent exposure; his mind also affected. Biederbick, felon on fore finger, condition doubtful. Salor, lame back, but able to go out occasionally. Connell, very weak from reduced diet. Cross, frosted foot is improving. Bender complains frequently of soreness in his chest and lame joints.

A bounteous repast this morning with which everyone was well pleased, consisted of stewed seal skins and fox intestines, thickened with mouldy dog biscuit. Nothing in our cuisine department is ever wasted, not even the cleanings of fox intestines.

November 22nd.

Long and Frederik each shot a blue fox today. I walked along the ice-foot about the peninsula in search of these little animals, but saw nothing. Standing on the highest point of the peninsula, I could discern the dark outline of the Greenland coast. To my intense satisfaction no water clouds were visible in that direction. We are hoping that the low temperature together with slack tides will close the sound early and provide a bridge for our deliverance from this horrible bondage.

Another stew this evening was thickened with the rotten dog biscuit. I believe that the meanest cur in the streets would have refused it, but to us it is life.

November 23rd.

Minimum temperature —41.5°. Long and Frederik each shot a fox again today.

November 24th.

All manner of schemes are being discussed. Ralston is trying to persuade some of his companions that they should join him in establishing a colony at Independence, Kansas. Rice and myself also have several visions which we intend to consider under more favorable circumstances. By way of entertainment, Fredericks, or Shorty as he is more familiarly called, gave us this evening a brief, interesting sketch of his life, prior to his entering the service. He is going to run a saloon in Minneapolis. Long wants to open a restaurant at Ann Arbor. Jewell thinks he would like to run the grocery in Ralston's colony.

SUNDAY, *November 25th.*

No water clouds in the direction of the Greenland coast renew our confidence in the freezing over of the sound at an early date and thus providing a means by which we can effect our escape as soon as the sun returns.

Hereafter Saturday evenings are to be set apart for the narration of personal histories. So far Fredericks' narration has provided the most enjoyable and interesting evening we have had.

Fred shot a large blue fox weighing four and a half pounds.

November 26th.

Temperature −36.5°.

Albert Head, Cape Camperdown and the remainder of Bache Island were distinctly outlined against the northern sky. Jens thinks that water exists near the middle of Kane Sea, but in the direction of Cairn Point he is of the opinion that it is frozen over. I climbed the hill to gain a view of the sound and consider the indications very favorable for our release if the cold weather continues with this marked absence of gales.

November 27th.

Minimum temperature −43.5°. A westerly wind, blowing at a velocity of twenty miles per hour, sprang up suddenly this evening.

I sent Fred to the summit of the little elevation above Camp Clay to observe the sound. He reports no water and the "Seco" is good; i.e. it is good travelling.

November 28th.

We are all looking forward to the Thanksgiving feast tomorrow; 3 lbs. rice, 2½ raisins, ½ lard, 1 can condensed milk, 1 can extract of coffee and 1½ can extract of chocolate were issued extra to both messes for the celebration. This Thanksgiving is vastly different from others within memory.

I find that a bag of bread which I had estimated at 70 pounds exceeded my estimate by 46 pounds. A seal also weighed 8 pounds more than I had estimated. These mistakes add days to our lives.

A new sort of entertainment this evening. Lieut. Lockwood proposed that each man make out a bill of fare which the Lieut. took down in shorthand. These menus are to be consolidated and a copy furnished each. If we are fortunate enough to escape with our lives, the members of the expedition will adhere as closely as possible to the bill of fare on their next birthdays.

November 29th.

The day was passed pleasantly. In fact, I think with perfect sincerity I may say that it has been the most enjoyable of my life. A double ration of coffee for breakfast will always be held in grateful remembrance. At 2:30 p.m. a fox stew with bacon was served after which rice pudding, chocolate and 7 ounces of hard bread were issued to each of us.

Twenty-five gills of rum and twelve lemons were used by Fredericks in making a punch which was pronounced the best of its kind. For the first time since the 1st inst. we had a feeling of repletion after eating. After the punch songs and stories filled the time until midnight. We then retired happier and more hopeful than for months.

November 30th.

Snow has been falling all day. A disagreeable drip from the roof is making our situation anything but pleasant. The party is feeling somewhat dull today. Perhaps it is because we were too well fed yesterday. If that is the source of our dullness, we will be troubled thus seldom.

December 1st.

This evening the wind veered around to the east and blew with great velocity, shaking our house to its foundation and driving the flying snow into the interior of our dwelling. Worse yet it opened the sound as far north as Cape Albert.

The drip continues from the roof and our sleeping

bags are wet through. We suffer much since the water has even penetrated our clothing.

Elison's hands and feet will have to be amputated. He bears his trouble with martyr-like fortitude and I think this has had a good effect on the others.

SUNDAY, *December 2nd.*

The high wind of last evening increased to a gale. Momentarily we were expecting our only protection—the boat—to be carried away. The snow driving under the edges covered the six men in my section to a depth of over a foot. I will long remember this most miserable night. The roof of the vestibule blew away and the tunnel has filled with snow. The pieces of wood taken from the whale-boat and piled outside have been scattered in all directions. Also the thermometer was blown away and lost. This starvation diet has made us so weak that we will be some time restoring order, if we ever can.

This is our feast day—the day on which we eat hard-tack pudding. The mixture of bread and salt water is most delicious and, best of all, filling. All during the entire week, we look forward to this satisfying dish with pleasant expectations. . . .

December 4th.

Brisk westerly winds have been howling over our house since yesterday. This evening they were accompanied by snow and heavy drift. A great expanse of water exists in Smith Sound, if dense water clouds indicate correctly. Our chances of crossing to Littleton Island on the ice are slowly narrowing, but we cling to the hope that somehow it can be done. Our conversation, as usual, is of food, since over all our other miseries, hunger predominates. We never tire of this sort of talk.

The invalids are mending slowly.

Our energy appears to have deserted us. But is a man supposed to possess energy when means of sustaining life is denied him? I think not. Notwithstanding the lack of energy for work, some have developed remarkably as grumblers. Making all due allowance for our condition, little fault should be found with the free expression of these morbid minds. And besides, pent-up feelings might be injurious to the general health.

A highly flavored stew of fox intestines and seal skin was enjoyed and favorably commented on by all this evening.

December 5th.

A gale broke suddenly on us at 3 a.m. It subsided at noon and the sky cleared beautifully, but in
the evening the wind rose again with greater fury
and once more threatened to demolish our quarters.
The door was snowed up, the vestibule blown down
and the commissary storehouse damaged considerably. Just before noon we were not able to see 30
yards ahead in the blinding drift. I issued nothing
today except the necessary bread.

Temperature at 1 p.m. 7°.

December 6th.

These storms have caused a disintegration of the
floe even to the ice-foot in the little cove west of
camp. From the hill I observed numerous pools
and lanes in all directions, and dark water clouds
hover over Smith Sound extending far to the northward beyond Cape Camperdown. The turbulent pack,
grinding and grumbling, as if contending for suprem-
acy of the waters, produces a mournful, rumbling
sound which strikes terror to the heart of the listener.

Long was fortunate enough to shoot a three pound
fox before breakfast.

December 7th.

Brisk westerly wind. Temperature −21°.

The moon appeared this afternoon and shining down through the clear atmosphere produced a very pretty effect on the desolate country.

The water hole in our lake has been neglected for several days and was entirely closed this morning. Rice and I with great effort cut it through again. Everyone is weak; also disheartened, since the channel ice has been broken up by the wind. For several days past I have been trying to get the vestibule repaired, but in vain.

December 8th.

The pack appears to be in great commotion again today. There was scarcely a moment that it could not be heard crashing against the rocky point of our peninsula and tumbling about outside as the currents whirled it swifty along.

The party worked in the vestibule this morning clearing away the snow and debris.

Tonight I killed two blue foxes at the same time. Rather good for darkness and indifferent marksmanship.

SUNDAY, *December 9th.*

Long shot two foxes this morning. These, together with those killed by me yesterday, weigh 13⅜ pounds. This furnishes meat ration for over two days.

A fine stew of hard bread and salt water was relished this morning. A thin, watery seal meat stew for dinner would have made us supremely happy had there been a greater quantity of it. These hot drinks and warm stews appear to be the one source of life to us. Taken cold they would not be nearly so effective in repelling the dampness and frost.

December 10th.

A westerly gale blowing all day and our condition miserable in consequence. Temperature −27°.

The party confined themselves closely to their sleeping bags and discussed the latest incongruous combination of hash.

December 11th.

The wind subsided during the morning, the sky cleared, and the day turned out beautifully clear.

No water clouds were visible to the north or east.

Vestibule repaired. I worked nearly four hours and then was overcome by dizziness. I started to faint, but quickly revived when I fell against the sledge.

Several of the men are entirely out of tobacco and the deprivation is going hard with them. They are willing to exchange their food for it. I am thankful now, if never before, that I care nothing for tobacco in any form.

December 12th.

I issued the weekly supply of rations this morning. This is an irksome task. My fingers have been frost-bitten so frequently that they are very sore and tender. Standing a long time in the low temperature of the commissary storehouse and handling the brass cartridges used as weights, my hands and feet become numb and my body thoroughly chilled.

Accusations were made against Fredericks, the cook, by Dr. Pavy and others of an unjust division of the stew. I believe Fredericks innocent. Other members of the mess will hereafter make the division.

December 13th.

These disheartening winds continue. Nothing done outside today. Inside—geographical sketches of the United States by Lieut. Greely. . . .

December 15th.

The beauty of the moon's halo today was doubly enhanced by the hazy atmosphere through which we viewed it.

The water hole on the lake was again frozen up. Through the energy of Ellis it was recut.

I visited the old camp in search of foxes, but met with no success. The flag planted by Rice and myself was blown down and the staff broken.

A stew of fox intestines, hearts, livers, lungs, etc. together with a small quantity of seal skin gave us a most satisfactory breakfast.

SUNDAY, *December 16th.*

High wind which caused a blinding drift made us wretched, confined as we were in the limited space of the damp sleeping bags.

Dr. Pavy tells me Elison will lose all his fingers and one of his feet. The amputation, however, can be postponed until we reach Littleton Island in March.

A hard bread pudding, rich with rice, raisins and seal blubber, made us comparatively happy in our stomachs. Although I am no smoker, the two cigarettes given me by Lieut. Kislingbury after breakfast were greatly enjoyed. Half a gill of rum and one quarter of a lemon to each man is issued regularly on Sunday.

December 17th.

I cleared the snow from the vestibule this morning. No one was willing to assist except Rice. He is always ready to do as much for others as for himself. Long and Fredericks are cooks for the two messes and, of course, are never allowed to perform any of the outside work. Unless some of the men exhibit more ambition, they will never be able to save their lives when we attempt to cross Smith Sound. I am very weak, but cannot refrain from working as long as I am able to move about.

This afternoon while working outside, my strength left me and complete prostration followed. I was once so strong and self-reliant that it seems almost incredible that my strength has been diminished until it scarcely equals that of a child. Tears spring unbidden to my eyes when I look on my emaciated features in our mirror, or when I feel my shrunken muscles.

December 18th.

This is a beautiful evening, the stars scintillating and sparkling in their setting of deepest azure, nowhere more brilliant than in the Arctic.

During our continuous discussions of food nearly all reproach themselves for not having eaten more when they had the opportunity. No one appears to recollect ever having disliked any dish of which he has partaken.

December 19th.

I issued the rations for the coming week. When volunteers are called for to perform certain odd jobs necessary to health and comfort, no one responds except Rice, Salor and occasionally Schneider. Cross saws and prepares wood for the cooks. We will need more energy than this in the party, if we are to save ourselves.

Elison's feet are black, shrunken and lifeless. His ankles are a horrible sight. The flesh has sloughed away leaving the bones devoid of covering. He suffers much, but is very patient and bears his troubles with fortitude.

December 20th.

Fred shot a white fox which weighed $4\frac{1}{8}$ pounds.

Another spring tide has just passed and this time the ice in Smith Sound was probably not broken. At least, there is no indication of open water toward the Greenland coast. This is certainly cheering and will serve to infuse new life and vigor in the torpid minds of a large number of the party. There is much speculation of what is in store for us at Littleton Island.

I find that my estimates of bread and meat were too low. Consequently the provisions will be extended several days further than anticipated. In the issue this week instead of the usual seal skin for stews, the flipper and intestines of Long's last seal were used. These will be augmented by the delicious (?) intestines of foxes and a small quantity of the mouldy hard bread.

December 21st.

There is still no indication of open water in Smith Sound. The natives think that the ice is most likely in good condition for travelling. They inspire us with hope by assurances of game when the sun returns.

This is the 27th anniversary of my birth. Also the winter solstice occurs at 10 p.m.

At my home today they are probably discussing my fate and perhaps mourn me as lost forever. How I wish that I could relieve their minds!

I shot a fox which weighed three pounds and twelve ounces. There are evidently two distinct breeds as the white ones weigh nearly two pounds more than the blue. Some, however, think there is only one kind, that a change is gradually taking place in the blue foxes and they are turning from blue to a dingy white or gray.

We keep a strict account of the intestines and issue them alternately to each mess. The heart and liver are the perquisite of the hunter. As an incentive to the natives, an ounce of tobacco is given them whenever they succeed in shooting a fox.

Lieut. Kislingbury was kind enough to give me a

cigarette which I smoked while drinking my birthday rum.

December 22nd.

The sky has been wondrously clear and bright and not a breath of air stirring. Temperature −29°.
We remained quietly in our bags all day, meditating on the probable fate of our forlorn party.

A stew of mouldy hard bread and one can of ox tail soup made a rich dish for our mess of twelve. At Fort Conger ten cans of this same soup were required to begin dinner.

SUNDAY, *December 23rd.*

The Doctor informs us that the prospects for Elison's recovery are favorable. He will lose all his fingers and the greater part of his feet.

Many complain their feet are sore and swollen to such an extent that they are almost deprived of their use. The frosted feet of Henry and Cross do not appear to improve much. Warmth and nourishment are now needed to infuse new life in the emaciated frames of our sufferers.

The poor cooks retired at an early hour this evening, both ill from inhaling smoke caused by burning damp wood. While the meals are being cooked, our room is filled with dense smoke which nearly suffocates us. All except the cooks can protect themselves by crawling down in their bags.

I exchanged half of my hard bread pudding this morning for half of one of the others next Sunday morning. We have frequently resorted to this method to secure a good meal at one time. There is a drawback, however. It is necessary to go hungry that we may feast tomorrow.

Whisler has been particularly disagreeable today and not at all choice in his use of language toward his companions. His frequent invitations to go out and fight have not been accepted. Under the circumstances, he is not to blame for what he said. Everyone is more or less cranky and I only wonder that we are not insane. All including myself are sullen and at times very surly.

December 24th.

By direction of Lieut. Greely I made extra issues for Christmas as follows: 3 pounds rice, 2½ raisins, 2 blubber, 1 lard, 4 hard bread dust, ½ sugar, 6 lemons, 1½ can cloud berries and 12 gills rum.

Dr. Pavy is suffering with nervous chills. We are greatly alarmed over his illness for without medical skill we would be in a deplorable situation.

December 25th.

A Merry Christmas!

Weather clear and calm. Temperature −35.5°. Lieut. Kislingbury's 36th birthday.

Our bill of fare today was substantially the same as on Thanksgiving except an increase of one ounce of bread to each man. The best of good feeling prevailed and three cheers were given for Lieut. Greely, Elison, Rice and the cooks. The records from Brevoort Island found by Rice in October were read again to the satisfaction of all. I predict that Lieut. Garlington will visit us during the full moon of January. The rum punch brewed by Fredericks and Long was the best that I have ever tasted. Our only regret—there was not more of it. Strange to say everyone felt full and satisfied.

I went over to our old camp and replaced the broken flag staff. No water clouds were visible in the direction of the Greenland coast. This fact strengthens our hope of being able to reach the coast of Greenland during March or that assistance may come to us.

The evening until after 10 o'clock was devoted to songs in which the two Eskimos joined with their peculiar, sweet native melodies and Danish songs. The spirits of the party are wonderfully joyous. If we continue as now, there will be little danger of losing our minds.

What a contrast is ours to the Spitzbergen party of walrus hunters who, although with an abundance of food, did not have a single survivor owing to the depressed spirits and their use of salt food instead of fresh when plenty of the latter was to be had. Much praise is due Lieut. Greely for all the entertainment he manages to provide for us. The diversions keep us hopeful.

[Christmas at Cape Sabine as described by Lieutenant Lockwood in his diary:

"December 25.— . . . It was agreed that we should give each of the two Eskimos fifty cents from each member of the expedition, to be kept for them until next Christmas.

"December 26.—Yesterday has passed, but I find

my notes of yesterday very imperfect. The day was a great success. We all had enough, or nearly enough . . . It was agreed early in the morning that nothing should be said to mar the pleasure of the day. Many kindly thoughts were expressed for those at home, and oh! how often we spoke of what was going on at our several homes. Many of the party gave the bill of fare at homes . . . Invitations to future Christmases—arrangements for future Christmas meetings . . . The reading of the records. Some songs in all languages, including French, German, Danish, and Greenland. . . . The punch was extremely fine. Chocolate about 7 o'clock, and by this time most of us were too full for utterance. . . .

"We have all been feeling extremely well all day, nice and warm and comfortable in the extreme. Several of us ate too much yesterday . . . but we all slept well . . . Our talk this morning was of home and our families . . . I spoke this morning of the reunions of my family, and how enjoyable they were. The remarks about my father brought tears—the first time I have shed tears in this country, if I except the occasion at Eskimo Point, when Rice returned with the Garlington records—the only time. I spoke also

of my sisters and of Mary Murray, whose many virtues I eulogized highly. . . . Kislingbury was kind
enough to make for each of the party a cigarette. . . ."

After Lieutenant Lockwood's death Shoe Island
which he discovered near the Farthest North, was re-
named Mary Murray Island.]

December 26th.

Owing to our dissipation of yesterday no one
awoke until 7 o'clock.

I issued the weekly supply of provisions this morning. Foxes were issued in lieu of seal for two days.
If our fuel and water should give out we can eat the
seal meat raw.

We were made happy (comparatively) this morning, with a stew of seal tail or flipper with fox intestines and mouldy hard bread.

I shot a 3 pound 2 ounce fox this evening.

December 27th.

Temperature −39.5°. A cold raw day.

Rice has volunteered for the hazardous duty of
visiting Littleton Island on February 1st in quest of

Lieut. Garlington, and we had a long discussion over the matter last evening. The talks have a beneficial effect by engaging the mind and turning it from gloomy reflections. During these general conversations many suggestions are made and we always come away feeling more hopeful than before. It is wonderful how calmly and quietly all discuss our almost certain fate if no assistance comes from Littleton Island.

Fredericks tells me that in his opinion Elison brought the dire disaster of losing his limbs on himself. He was detected several times injudiciously eating snow during the trip to Cape Isabella in the low temperature of November. Linn also came near falling a victim of the same indiscreet act. I am surprised that Elison did this as he had before his eyes the experiences of all previous expeditions. [Also, it was a point of honor with the men to refrain from eating snow while on sledging trips in low temperatures.]

December 28th.

Weather clear with light westerly winds. Temperature —35°.

To eke out our scanty supply of fuel, we began using a small quantity of tarred rope in conjunction with the barrel staves. The trial was quite successful, but the dense smoke was almost unbearable.

I began issuing the frozen bread left in the wreck cache by Lieut. Garlington. The fox stews are not at all satisfactory because of the great number of bones. Its value is full 50 per cent less than seal meat. Fearing that our fuel will not last as long as the provisions, Lieut. Greely directed me to issue ten pounds of blubber to the cooks for an experiment. Lieut. Lockwood objected to this and a very disagreeable discussion at once ensued. The Lieut. is weakening under the strain.

December 29th.

The greater portion of the day was spent in making bargains for the exchange of food. It was, in fact, a regular marketing day.

Cross and Bender have been excused by the Doctor from the performance of any duty. The frost-bitten foot of the former is much worse.

I dug out of the snow the last of the whale-boat and it will be burned at once.

SUNDAY, *December 30th.*

In the marketing yesterday I secured the hard bread pudding of another man. With my own allowance this made quite a satisfactory meal and placed me on better terms with myself. I lay nearly all day in a dreamy, listless state thinking of home and friends, and wondering if this living death with all its attendant horrors will ever end.

Today completes half of the time that we expect to remain here, calculating from November 1st when final reduction in provisions took place. If at the end of the next 60 days, the party generally is in as good condition as now, we expect to squeeze through.

Gun-powder has been substituted to a certain extent for salt—five pounds of it having been found in the wreck cache.

December 31st.

The water hole gave out this morning and another was completed at 4:30 p.m. with only three inches of water at the bottom of the lake.

I wonder if the time will ever come when I will not be restricted in the amount of food that I wish to consume! This craving, the continual gnawing at my stomach, is horrible. It brings with it visions of the most tempting dishes.

January 1st, 1884.

We enter the new year under particularly favorable conditions, when one considers the true nature of our situation. The health of the party is generally good. The provisions are turning out excellently, all estimates having been too low. The wound in the sound appears to have frozen over as no water clouds are visible. Everyone feels hopeful of deliverance before our rations are exhausted.

I visited our old camp in search of foxes. I fired at one but did not secure him. The short walk left me exhausted.

I made an extra issue of a few articles for the feast today. Most of us were awake at midnight to greet the New Year. How are our friends spending the day? Do they think us alive? Temperature −32°.

January 2nd.

Jens reports having heard the grinding of the moving pack in Buchanan Strait this morning. I sincerely hope that the break is not general.

Elison's right foot dropped off this morning with-out his knowledge. One of his fingers fell off a few days ago and several others will follow in a short time. Ralston is quite ill. Biederbick having over-eaten yesterday now suffers with cramp in his stom-ach.

Compared with two weeks ago, there is already a marked difference in the light furnished by the reflec-tion of the distant sun.

January 3rd.
Temperature –31°.

The moon produced a very pretty effect on the ice-bergs this evening when it rose above the extremity of Cape Sabine.

January 4th.
On entering the commissary storehouse this morn-ing, I found a hole cut through the canvas roof and about one-quarter pound of bacon missing.

January 5th.
This morning I discovered that another hole had been cut in the canvas of the commissary storehouse

and carefully covered by snow blocks. I think the thief is one of two men whom I am watching closely. I gave notice this morning that I had set a spring gun among the provisions and that any man who interfered with them did so at the risk of his life. I really did not set the gun, but left the party, except Lieut. Greely, in ignorance of that fact.

Elison's remaining foot dropped off this morning.

SUNDAY, *January 6th.*

The cook [Fredericks] in my mess reported that someone had been tampering with the bacon which I issued on Thursday. On examination I found marks of a knife and about four ounces of the piece missing.

The usual Sunday issue of rum and lemon was made this afternoon. Jewell became possessed of two dishes of hard bread pudding this morning by driving sharp bargains during the "marketing" hours. In eating both he made himself sick.

January 7th.

This morning I discovered that one of the barrels of English hard bread had been broken into and about 5 pounds of bread stolen. The mark of an axe was found where the staves had been crushed. Since I know the person who was working in the vicinity of this barrel a few days ago and had in his possession this particular axe, I have no trouble in locating the thief to my own satisfaction. But I shall need more evidence before making an accusation against him. Repeated calls were made for the thief to come forward and openly acknowledge his guilty action. As a further inducement all the others offered to contribute a piece of bread from their scanty store that he might never again be tempted.

We can hear the ice moving in Buchanan Strait but Fred says the open space is probably not extensive.

January 8th.

Lieut. Greely offered me an increase of one ounce of bread per day over the others, on account of the irksome duties which I have to perform. Although weak and sadly in need of it, I refused on the ground of injustice to my comrades. I will take my chances with them.

A fine stew of seal for dinner. All cares and troubles vanished for a few hours.

January 9th.

Rice returned from a visit to the hill and reported a misty atmosphere over the sound which would seem to point to the presence of open water. Fred and myself went on the hill and saw evidence of the mischief done the floe by the late storms. Vapor was rising in dense clouds from the many fissures in the pack and noises made by the moving ice could be distinctly heard. This is indeed a bitter disappointment as the disruption may prevent us from reaching Littleton Island.

It is just five months today since we abandoned Fort Conger to begin the retreat southward. Now is a fine time to travel owing to the good weather which has prevailed for several days past. Will assistance come to us this moon, I wonder?

Our stock of tobacco has nearly all disappeared. Birch bark and tea leaves have been substituted by the smokers. Fred drives us nearly crazy by smoking old rags.

January 10th.

Ellis complaining of illness. His speech is greatly affected by the excessive use of dried tea leaves and birch bark. Dr. Pavy has prohibited him and Ralston from smoking. Cross and Schneider who have been lying down constantly for several days, except when roused for meals, were ordered by Lieut. Greely to sit up at least two hours each day.

Rice has explained to Jens that he is to accompany him on the journey to Littleton Island in February. The faithful native appeared deeply touched that he should have been selected for this important and hazardous duty. . . .

January 12th.

Lockwood is very weak. He has been saving the greater portions of his bread and meat for several days and talks to himself about food. For hours he stares at the lamp and frequently requests that it be kept burning during the night. Biederbick who sleeps next to him believes that his mind is going.

This is Elison's thirty-fourth birthday. We were all indebted to him this evening for a cigarette which he asked us to smoke in commemoration of the event. It is just two months since the brave fellow was brought in here from what seems almost certain death.

Orders have been issued by Lieut. Greely prohibiting the use of tea leaves as a substitute for tobacco.

Lieut. Greely directed me to increase the bread ration to 6 ounces per man per day. It is now 5½ ounces. The change although slight is welcome.

SUNDAY, *January 13th.*

Lockwood continues petulant. He talks a great deal to himself about his favorite dishes. Ellis, Linn, Ralston, Cross and Jewell are also badly broken down in strength. They seldom leave their bags unless coerced.

Rum and lemon with half an ounce extra bread made this a great day.

One barrel will scarcely suffice for three days fuel. At this rate we have sufficient for over two months more. . . .

January 15th.

Rice made his first preparations today for his journey to Littleton Island by cutting off the extra dog skin on Dr. Pavy's sleeping bag for stockings.

Our tea has been reduced to one-half pint per man per meal.

January 16th.

Cross is growing weak. He has failed greatly since yesterday morning. I think he is near the end.

Whisler claims that he detected the Doctor purloining bread from Elison's dish. The Doctor sleeps by the side of Elison and keeps the bread can under his own charge feeding Elison when he needs it.

January 17th.

Temperature −36°.

Cross is failing rapidly. He talks incoherently of his mother, of his birthday (next Sunday) when he will be forty years of age, and of the returning sun.

Jens believes that the sound is broken and considerable water space exists.

Lieut. Greely has named February 2nd as the day on which Rice and Jens will begin their journey to Littleton Island in quest of assistance.

January 18th.

Temperature −39°. This is what the thermometer registered, but the mercury was frozen and so we have no means of knowing how much colder it was. The returning light is quite well marked.

Cross grew worse during the night and at 1:45 p.m. breathed his last, passing away quietly. He had been unconscious since dinner yesterday. He will be buried tomorrow noon on the low gravelly ridge which separates Camp Clay from the *Proteus* wreck cache. As we cannot spare wood for a coffin, I suggested wrapping him in a large gunny sack which I had in the commissary storehouse. He died from dropsical effusion of the heart and had slight symptoms of scurvy. At least, this is the official version of his death, undoubtedly presented to spare the feelings of our undernourished crew.

In a few well-chosen words, Lieut. Greely spoke of the past life of the deceased. He called attention to the fact that our duty now is to the living, pointing out particularly that this should not be an occasion for depression. Biederbick has been unremitting in his attentions to Cross during the last hours of his illness.

On visiting the hill, I saw dense water clouds of vapor hanging over Smith Sound. This is surely bad for Rice's contemplated trip.

January 19th.

Clear and calm. Mercury frozen again.

The remains were dressed for burial by Biederbick and myself, and wrapped in a large gunny sack.
Lieut. Greely read the beautiful Episcopal burial
service while we were yet in our sleeping bags, and
about noon the solemn procession moved slowly
across the lake and up the gentle incline to the grave.
The body was covered with the Stars and Stripes and
was borne on the small sledge which already has a
history in connection with the Elison disaster last
fall. We carefully arranged a circle of stones about
the grave, this being the only attention we could be-
stow on our comrade.

One cannot conceive of anything more unearthly—
more weird and solemn—than this ghostly procession of emaciated men moving slowly and silently
away from their wretched ice-prison in the uncertain
light of the Arctic night, having in their midst a dead
comrade about to be laid away forever in the frozen
ground. It was a scene that I can never forget.

The bread ration has been increased to seven and
a half ounces.

SUNDAY, *January 20th.*
Mercury is lost sight of in the bulb.

A splendid hard bread pudding in the morning and a beautiful stew of seal meat in the evening—joy! We gloat over the Sunday bill of fare as if it were a feast instead of a wretched mess of the vilest compound.

Lockwood is growing weaker and weaker. His fitful moods almost break my heart. As I watch him, tears gather in my eyes and there is a lump of sorrow which almost bursts my throat. That this should be the strong, daring and enthusiastic Lockwood with whom I went to the "Farthest."

He said to me a few days ago, "Brainard, I have lost my grip." Pitiful, pitiful. It's true, too. He has lost the last hope of life.

Psalms were read this morning, and the usual issue of rum and lemon made.

January 22nd.

The condition of Lieut. Lockwood is unchanged. Since he is the weaker of the two now, Lieut. Kislingbury returned the mattress which Lockwood had loaned him last fall.

Owing to the rapidly increasing light very few stars were visible at noon. . . .

January 24th.

Lockwood appears to be improving slightly under the late increase of rations. The social barometer has certainly risen several inches in the last two days. Raw bacon—or as Whisler puts it, "Prairie Fish"—was again issued this morning.

A chronological table of all the principal events of the world was introduced by Lieut. Greely this evening and proved very interesting to all. Dr. Pavy who has a remarkable memory and is full of information, supplies whatever we lack in the way of dates.

January 25th.

A fine stew of seal meat made us all rejoice this evening.

I have watched the sound very closely this winter and I believe it is open at the present time. I will not speak of that to the men who think it frozen. Better their minds remain in a hopeful state.

Biederbick is 25 years old today.

January 26th.

Our supper of English canned beef and dog biscuit was enjoyed by all. The increase of rations to

Rice and Jens to put them in condition for their journey to the Greenland coast began today.

Eskimo Fred celebrated his 37th birthday.

Jewell has been conducting himself like a child during the last few days. With hunger slowly consuming his life, the poor fellow cannot be blamed for saying foolish things occasionally.

SUNDAY, *January 27th.*

A beautiful day. Clear, calm and a glorious light in the southern sky which promises the early return of the sun. Temperature −36°.

The Doctor began treating the feet of Rice and Jens so that they might be better able to withstand the low temperature.

Three white foxes were seen.

January 28th.

Lieut. Greely stated to me in confidence that as Lockwood's mind is growing weak, Lieut. Kislingbury would take command in the event of any disaster overtaking him (Lieut. Greely). The Doctor said that if Lockwood did not brace up he would never recover. . . .

January 31st.

I put up six days rations for Rice and Jens to take with them. Lieut. Greely has prepared a record for Rice to deposit on Littleton Island in the event of his meeting no one there. He has also made out a short list of provisions which he desires brought over by the relief party, provided a relief party is there. Dr. Pavy has also furnished a list of medicines of the kind most needed now.

Lockwood, poor fellow, is not improving. I think I can see death in his eyes.

February 1st.

The outfit for Rice's journey is now complete and he will start tomorrow morning if the weather permits.

Lieut. Lockwood is no better. I wish he would try to be more cheerful.

February 2nd.

The cooks were called at 4:45 a.m. to enable Rice and Jens to start early. They left at 8:45 a.m. Fred and myself took their packs and started ahead in order to give them a good lift at the beginning of their journey. The weight of their packs averages about fifty pounds each. They overtook us before we had gone far. A tremulous "God bless you" a hasty pressure of their hands and we turned away in tears from those brave souls who are daring and enduring so much for us. We waited until their receding forms were lost to view in the bewildering confusion of the ice-fields and then slowly retraced our steps to the hut.

While watching their progress, I distinctly heard the hoarse grinding of the moving pack not far away. Of this I said nothing to my companions on returning. I believe that Rice will be turned back by water and his heroic efforts in our behalf thus rendered fruitless.

After the exertion this morning I was prostrated with a nervous chill, but was revived somewhat by aromatic spirits of ammonia and rum.

Long was fortunate enough to shoot a blue fox which will furnish us with almost a meal.

Lockwood seems somewhat better. Fred astounded us all by announcing his intentions of committing suicide. He is probably feeling lonely since the departure of Jens.

SUNDAY, *February 3rd.*

Light westerly wind in the morning which increased almost to a gale toward evening. Poor Rice! We are all thinking about him and Jens exposed to the full fury of this storm.

Jewell fell down in a dead faint this evening. Connell also has been feeling unwell. The exposure and exertion of yesterday has left me in anything but an agreeable condition. I caught a cold which has settled in all my joints and muscles, and my face and hands are greatly swollen.

February 4th.

Temperature −24.5°. The thermometer was read at noon by the light from the returning sun.

I feel no better today. The Doctor seemed alarmed at my condition, but I cannot imagine it serious. Lockwood got up today and moved about without assistance. Biederbick is now in excellent condition, notwithstanding he has worked unremittingly in the interests of the sick. When he left Fort Conger he could scarcely walk on account of rheumatism. In the face of dampness, hunger, and exposure, he has steadily improved in health. . . .

February 6th.

As I had predicted, Rice and Jens returned having met with open water about two miles east of Brevoort Island. They followed along the water's edge to the southward until opposite Baird Inlet, expecting to find some point that was bridged over by the ice. At every turn they met with bitter disappointments and were at last compelled to give up.

Both of them passed last night in agony. Jens frosted his fingers in the sleeping bag and Rice had to thaw them out in contact with his own warm body. They were compelled to get up and run about in the snow to keep from freezing until there was sufficient light for travelling. Jens is badly broken down and Rice is not far behind him. Their lamp proved ineffective and for two days they had scarcely a swallow of water. Rice believes that he travelled 50 miles in all on this trip.

February 7th.

Rice and Jens are sore and stiff in their joints, but are better than we had expected they would be.

Lieut. Greely says that he will try to remain here until March 6th and, if the sound is not closed then,

there will be little probability of its closing. Our
remaining stores may prolong our lives till April.

February 8th.

Mercury again frozen. It has been a beautiful
day.

Notwithstanding the improbability of our reaching
the Greenland coast next month, preparations for
the trip will go actively forward. Boards were appointed by Lieut. Greely to attend to all details.

It is just six months since we left Fort Conger. . . .

SUNDAY, *February 10th.*

Temperature −36.5°.

Both meals were very fine today and for a short
time all were comparatively happy.

On the authority of an inventory just completed
we can remain here until March 12th on our present
ration, and then have ten days full rations with which
to cross to Littleton Island.

February 11th.

I visited the hill this morning and could hear the
crushing of the pack in Buchanan Strait very dis-

tinctly. It sounded like thunder and made me
tremble. Our lives depend on its quiescent state.
The heavy water clouds were unnecessary to indicate
the presence of much water.

Are those clouds an augury of our future? I fear
so. Without firm ice for crossing to Littleton Island
slight hopes for life remain to us.

The words of Lieut. Garlington after the crushing
of the *Proteus* by the ice that "everything within the
power of man will be done to rescue the brave men
at Fort Conger from their perilous position," brought
tears to the eyes of the men who listened to the reading of the record that night in October in our dimly
lighted hut at Eskimo Point. The words inspired us
with hope then, but I am afraid the promise was
made lightly and without a full knowledge of the
difficulties to be encountered.

Difficulties! And more than mere difficulties!
Since our water hole gave out a month ago, we have
not had drinking water and we cannot spare the fuel
with which to melt ice. Several of the men begged
for water today, but there is not a man among us with
strength enough to find and start another fresh water
hole. Lieut. Lockwood was so pitifully persistent in

his plea for water that Lieut. Greely finally melted him some ice in the warmth of his sleeping bag.

In estimating the weights to be carried if we cross the sound, Rice and I found that they would total about 1,600 pounds. Nearly all joined in the discussion this morning relative to our equipment for the trip. Lieut. Greely directed me to issue stockings and mittens to those in need of them. I issued the last of the seal meat and also the remainder of the American bacon.

In emptying the rum keg I found it about two gallons short. The mistake was made in issuing with an English measure instead of the U. S. measure which is smaller.

February 12th.

The temperature is very low. The mercury is frozen and we judge it to be about −50°.

Rice reports having a good view of the sound from Cemetery Ridge and seeing a large space of water. The noise made by the crushing ice can be distinctly heard in our camp. Even after all the dangers and hardships through which we have passed, I do not think that I am inclined to look on the gloomy side of our prospects. Nevertheless, if the channel will not permit us to cross and no help comes from the opposite side, we are all dead men in a few weeks more.

February 13th.

I issued stockings to the party and made the usual weekly issue of rations. The last of our rice went today. The provisions will extend to March 12th at least.

Fredericks began the irksome duty of repairing our seal skin boots. It tries his fingers greatly.

February 14th.

The water appears to be encroaching steadily on the ice about Cape Sabine. The clouds caused by this increasing space are less marked than before. No Valentine will make its appearance this year if the ice can prevent it.

My hunger today has made me think more and more of food. All sorts of incongruous combinations have flashed through my head and I have not been able to refrain from discussing them all around the hut.

A small piece of butter was found missing from a can sitting on the shelf in the boat. Henry keeps his candle moulds on the same shelf.

February 15th.

Lieut. Lockwood is better, but he does not improve as rapidly as we would wish.

The sun will appear above the horizon tomorrow for the first time, if the temperature should fall to −50°. We do not enthuse much over the return, but each one thinks more than he cares to express in words.

Schneider, Ellis and Salor are sewing on boots, stockings, mittens, etc. for the crossing to Greenland. Fredericks and Jens perform the most important portion of the work on the boots.

A few moments spent at our meals are the most pleasant of the day. As we eat, we are for the moment satisfied within and our relations with one another all around become a little more friendly. For the most part, the party appears to be doing well on the reduced rations just at present. All except Bender.

Time is passing wearily.

February 16th.

We were not favored by seeing the sun above the horizon owing to the high temperature. Neither could its reflection be seen on Bache Island.

I looked over the shotgun ammunition today. We have 265 rounds, only 25 of which will do for seals and larger game.

SUNDAY, *February 17th.*

According to Israel's calculations, the sun at noon was 10° above the horizon. It was not visible to us because of the dark water clouds. The sun has been absent 115 days. In the future, if we have any, we intend remaining where it can be seen once in every twenty-four hours.

Owing to the limited quantity of rum on hand, no more will be issued for the present, except for sickness.

February 18th.

The last of our corned beef, seal meat, mutton, American bacon, seal skin, peas, string beans, carrots, salmon, bread found in the *Proteus* cache, bread brought from Fort Conger, English chocolate, Eng-

lish tea and sugar mixture, and onion powder, have
been issued; also all our salt and pepper, except a
small quantity kept for Elison's use.

Rice visited the summit of the island and on his
return reported Smith Sound a great sea with rafts
of ice drifting on the surface. If what Rice says is
true, I think we are doomed to die in this place but,
however horrible the end, most of us are prepared
to face it like men. Bender, though, would rather
consume all the provisions now and die, rather than
prolong them with the hope of rescue.

February 19th.

This afternoon I visited Cemetery Ridge and my
observations from that point confirmed Rice's report
that Smith Sound is an open sea. No ice of any description was visible on its surface. Waves and
white caps were rolling in against the edge of the
fast ice with a dismal roar. To my ears, the roar
sounded like the knell of our impending doom.

The water has encroached close to Cape Sabine
and extends north toward Cape Napoleon and toward the Greenland coast as far as I could see.
Greenland is out of our reach, I fear.

February 20th.

A raven was observed this morning flying over our camp. We have suffered too long to give way to superstition at this hour.

Bender repaired an alcohol can and one of our stew pots in a most artistic manner, considering the material at hand.

February 21st.

After a brief visit to the hill, Rice reports water spaces in Smith Sound northeast of Cape Sabine, but he also imparts the cheering information that the ice has bridged across the sound farther to the south and that means of escape may yet be furnished us. At this announcement, the mercurial temperaments instantly rose several degrees and care and suffering were for the moment forgotten. Cold, calm weather is all that is now required to cement firmly this newly formed bridge of drift ice.

I issued the last of the frozen bread today. Yesterday the remaining portion of the English beef was used.

The large sledge has been shovelled out from the drift to be repaired.

Dr. Pavy is entertaining us with lectures on the history of France.

February 22nd.

The advent of Washington's birthday anniversary was hailed with delight. In honor of the occasion, Lieut. Greely directed that the cooks depart from the usual routine and prepare a hard bread pudding for breakfast. The stew for each mess contained 20 ounces of lard. This amount of fat made the dish rich and agreeable. In the evening a stew of English beef and lime juice pemmican proved superior to anything that we have yet eaten. I issued the last of the *Proteus* tea this morning. . . .

SUNDAY, *February 24th.*

The usual issue of lemon was made, but no rum was served and its absence is deplored, since it seemed to hold life giving qualities.

I again observed the sound from Cemetery Ridge. Considerable water was visible and the bridge which had formed a few days ago has entirely disappeared under the influence of the late wind storms. This is something not wholly unexpected, but at the same time it is a bitter disappointment. I think, though, that we can bear pain and disappointments with greater fortitude than we could a few months ago.

The annoying dripping from the roof of our hut continues.

In a letter to the Commanding Officer, Lieut. Kislingbury offers to conduct a small party of the strongest to Littleton Island to secure relief in the event of the sound's freezing over. In the same letter he objects to any further increase in our meat ration until we have some means of augmenting our supply. For the information of the party, Lieut. Greely stated that he would start for Littleton Island at the first opportunity, but would never divide the command. . . .

February 27th.

Dense clouds of vapor are seen ascending from Smith Sound.

This place appears to be entirely deserted by all animal life now.

Remainder of blubber, onion pickles, dog biscuits, coffee and beef extracts issued today.

Henry's birthday.

February 28th.

Yesterday Biederbick reported Lieut. Lockwood for using tobacco despite the orders of Lieut. Greely and Dr. Pavy. Lockwood's mind is evidently so weak that he had forgotten both the orders and the fact that he had used tobacco. This is not his true nature for I know him to be honest. His health is not improving and daily his disposition becomes more irritable. His failure in this crisis is the saddest sight in our hut. . . .

March 1st.

While cleaning the shot-gun, Bender through neglect lost one of the important extra parts, but the gun can yet be used if care is exercised in handling it.

Lieut. Greely said last night that if circumstances were favorable, he would increase the provisions next Wednesday and start for Littleton Island on the following Monday.

Long has told me a good joke on the party. On Henry's birthday, Long forgot to add the allowance of tea while preparing dinner. He did not discover his mistake until after he had issued each a cup of hot water. No one detected the absence of the tea and Long, of course, did not care to acknowledge the omission. He said nothing about the matter to anyone until today.

I prepared a large piece of tin on which will be marked Cross's name, age and date of death and then erected over his grave. We would like to use a portion of our boat for this purpose, but cannot afford it. Lieut. Greely has named the little lake which so long supplied us with water, Lake Cross.

SUNDAY, *March 2nd.*

From my inventory the Commanding Officer has made careful calculations and says that at our present rate we can live until the first week in April. If no opportunity occurs for crossing to Littleton Island before the 16th inst., all hope of leaving this place must be abandoned. If we do not succeed in securing game, our end will not be far distant on April 15th.

On my recommendation the Commanding Officer appointed Fredericks a sergeant in general service vice Cross deceased. This is a fitting recognition for his excellent services this winter.

Bender's inventive genius is irrepressible. He has designed and manufactured several fine candlesticks which may be used for a double purpose, either for candles or for lamps. Schneider is making stearine candles. Fredericks is still working on the sleeping stockings.

March 4th.

Lieut. Greely reduced the bread issue to eight ounces per man. The remainder of the blubber, Hudson Bay and American pemmican was issued this afternoon.

March 5th.

I issued the last of the corn, soup, tomatoes, and the English evaporated potatoes.

March 6th.

I issued the last can of lard to the cooks. A small portion is being kept for Elison's wounds.

March 7th.

The sun was seen this morning by Rice for the first time since last October. He had to pay dearly for the glimpse of the rosy face of Old Sol, climbing the rugged sides of the island nearly to the summit.

Long ascended Beebe Point and, after taking a survey of the floe, proceeded to the northeast to open water one mile further along. Following along the water's edge to Brevoort Island, he found only a narrow belt of ice between the water and the island. He climbed to the summit of the island and, looking to the northeast and south, he saw open water extending as far as the eye could reach. A few pieces of debris ice were drifting along with the current.

Kislingbury went out to the large berg just north of Camp Clay and, breaking through the ice, narrowly escaped drowning. He returned to the hut with his clothing frozen as hard as iron.

There is considerable open water about the berg. It seems that it ought to be a paradise for seals in a few weeks. Rice saw a brace of ptarmigan on Cemetery Ridge, but before he could secure a gun they had disappeared.

I issued the last of the chocolate extract and cloud berries.

Bender has been very aggressive in his conduct today. He flatly contradicted Lieut. Greely, and in addition made a very extravagant and reckless use of profanity.

March 8th.

A gale rose suddenly from the southeast at about 2 a.m. and continued without intermission during the entire day. It is, I think, our severest storm yet.

The remainder of our rice and tomatoes were used for soup this morning.

Fredericks transformed a three-man sleeping bag into one for the use of two men. The poor fellow suffers greatly while working in the low temperature of the hut, but he never complains.

I broke up another barrel for fuel. Two staves suffice to prepare a meal. It may be necessary to reduce even this meagre allowance.

For the first time this winter, we had our hair cut. The cut was comfortable, if not artistic. Those wishing to be cropped crawled on their hands and knees to the foot of their sleeping bags, and held their heads in the alley-way. The tonsorial artist passed along the line armed with a huge pair of shears and devoted about ten seconds to each head. My hair was over six inches long.

SUNDAY, *March 9th.*

Lieut. Greely has decided to send Long and Eskimo

Fred with the small sledge and six days provisions to Alexandra Harbor to secure game. According to various explorers, there is an abundance there. I had volunteered with others for the trip, and felt confident that I would be selected. I am disappointed. In our weakened state, this is a journey of extraordinary danger and hardship. There could have been no better selection than Long and Eskimo Fred. . . .

March 11th.

This is one of the most beautiful days we have known in this place. The welcome rays of the sun flooded the exterior of our hut for the first time. Temperature at 6 a.m. −19.1°.

To facilitate Long's journey, Rice and Ellis hauled his sledge to the west end of Cocked Hat Island. They report travelling as good, but their excessive weakness would not permit them to go far. They returned in fair condition. Long and Eskimo Fred left the hut a short time after the departure of the sledge with the kindest wishes of their grateful companions whose eyes will perhaps never see them again. A raven was seen near Cocked Hat Island.

From the hill I saw no apparent change in the ice-fields since yesterday. With a few cold nights and no high winds, we may expect to see the sound sufficiently closed for our purposes. Without such conditions—well, we must wait for the ship—or die!

I had Jens lash the large sledge together this morning so that everything might be in readiness for an immediate start at the right moment.

The evening readings continue and the days are passed in noisy discussions on the important events of the day in Germany, and in imaginatively preparing elaborate combinations of that popular dish known as hash. Our subjects appear to be pretty well talked over and for hours at a time silence reigns supreme. . . .

March 14th.

Temperature −30.5°. The day has been bright and beautiful owing to the presence of the sun.

Long and Fred returned at 7 p.m. yesterday much exhausted and frost-bitten. They had been unable to get into the sleeping bag together as it froze. They had reached Cape Viele the first evening. The next morning they passed around the cape and entered

Alexandra Harbor. Finding no traces of game, they followed around the head of the deep bay of which the former is an inlet until Mount Carey was reached.

This they ascended and saw three capes, heretofore unknown to explorers. The more westerly one has been named Cape Francis Long.

After an absence of over fourteen hours, they returned to Cape Viele where their sledge and equipment had been left. Here Long was suddenly taken ill and for a brief period dispaired of ever again returning to camp. Only he alone was able to crawl into the frozen sleeping bag, and then had to lie in a cramped position. Meanwhile, his faithful companion walked up and down near him to prevent himself from freezing.

With the temperature so low, he could not remain long in the frozen bag without becoming helpless. He took a few drops of aromatic spirits of ammonia with a drink of hot rum. This partially restored him and they were shortly able to retrace their steps homeward, reaching Cape Clay after an arduous tramp of fourteen hours.

This has all been a sad disappointment since we had reason to expect much from Alexandra Harbor after the favorable reports of game made by the English. On the other hand, we are fortunate not to have lost Long in his brave attempt to provide this party with food. Arctic explorers do not venture out in such cold weather, but our men went and then with their strength less than half what it should be.

Lieut. Greely says that he is going to send Long out again in a few days and this time I will accompany him. We will probably be absent eight days and may cross Buchanan Strait to Bache Island. We must find game.

Elison says that the spell is broken and that we may expect plenty of game in the future. I shot three ptarmigans this morning; hence his remark. No portion of these birds, except the feathers, was wasted.

Rice has at last persuaded the Commanding Officer to permit him to go to Baird Inlet where the 140 pounds of frozen meat was abandoned last November at the time of the Elison fiasco.

Biederbick was promoted today to hospital steward. His appointment, of course, is subject to the approval of the War Department. . . .

SUNDAY, *March 16th.*

The sound looks still more favorable for crossing. If it continues to improve next week, I think escape is probable.

Long and Frederik went out to the open water this morning taking with them the kayak. They returned with four dovekies and report having seen and fired at a small seal. The dovekies are small but plump and are dressed in their winter clothing—white feathers with black tips.

If Rice can obtain the meat from Baird Inlet, we can live until May 1st or about that time without assistance from Greenland. Long's success this morning in hunting has had an excellent effect on the spirits of the party.

Lieut. Greely contemplates sending Jens and myself to Rice's Strait to look for seal and other game. I volunteered also to go down to Payer Harbor to hunt and observe our chances for future aspirations there. I proposed to Lieut. Greely this morning that we make an attempt to catch shrimps. If possible I will prepare a net tomorrow. I exposed a tempting bait on the rocks in the vicinity of our hut as an inducement for the raven to visit us and be shot.

While on the hill this morning, the sun shone out
of the mist and I lingered among the rocks enjoying
its warmth and radiance.   To borrow the words of
Dr. Kane on observing the sun after its absence all
winter, "It was like bathing in perfumed water."

March 17th.

The barometer is falling slowly.   There are
indications of a severe storm in the sound and probably much of our newly formed ice has been broken,
destroying our very last chance of escape to Littleton
Island.   After a week of good weather, during which
our hopes for escape had grown to almost certainty,
this end to all these bright anticipations is indeed
hard.   We have nothing now to look forward to each
day—only starvation.   My imagination refuses to
play with the thought that there is a relief party
eagerly waiting to rescue us.

Jens shot a ptarmigan this morning near the hut.
It weighed twenty ounces.   The dovekies average
about one pound each.

I invented and made an apparatus with which to
catch shrimps.   Rice will test it at Beebe Point tomorrow.

In overhauling the stores in the commissary room, I found ten ounces of English chocolate which had been overlooked in the darkness. It will be kept for issue to Elison from time to time as he may desire. His ration is now sixteen ounces of bread and six ounces of meat. He maintains wonderful control over his feelings and is ever cheerful. The ration of the party is from eleven to twelve ounces per day—no more!

March 18th.

The raven was observed investigating the fox skin which I had exposed on a rock, but escaped the aim of a shot-gun.

March 19th.

I find that the tallow about the English bacon to preserve it is in excess of the forty pounds marked on the can.

The reduction in our rations has again revived the old topic of conversation—food, and many hours are passed quite pleasantly in telling one another of the bills of fare that we would order, if we had the chance.

March 20th.

Fresh, westerly winds have caused much drift and made outside work trying and disagreeable. Temperature −20.5°. The barometer is about stationary.

Notwithstanding the wind, Rice visited Beebe Point to test the shrimp net which I made a few days ago. He succeeded in catching about two ounces of the minute crustaceans and says that with slight modifications of the net, the fishery can be made successful. This opens up another chance of life.

An owl and a raven were seen today. The former was taking flight toward the north.

Fred is not feeling well. The late trip with Long has taken all his energy and despondency seems to have overcome his usual happy disposition.

Linn is evidently losing his mind. Since the exposure last fall on the Cape Isabella trip when Elison was frozen, he has never been himself.

. At my suggestion Lieut. Greely has directed that the kayak be conveyed to the open water each morning by some member of the party, thus lightening the labors of the hunters who are doing all in their power to procure game for us.

March 21st.

I made a light dip net and also a large hook for fish. Gardiner has invented a dredge for sea weed with which we hope to increase our food supply.

Both the natives are very much swollen about the face and limbs. It is the same trouble I experienced a few weeks ago from over-exertion.

March 22nd.

Rice was quite successful at shrimp fishing today. He secured about six ounces and expects to get at least a quart tomorrow. I made two nets for him this evening using fox skins as bait. Dovekie legs are also excellent bait, and will be reserved from the stews for that purpose. The shrimps are very small—about the size of a half-grown fly. They are properly known as sea-fleas.

With the long pole I made to capture seaweed, Rice was not so successful. In fact, he gathered none, but we both believe that with slight modifications the pole will yet be useful.

If the day is favorable, I am going to visit Rosse Bay tomorrow to hunt seals. Lieut. Greely said this evening that if no game has been secured by the first

week in April, he will reduce rations to a basis which
will enable us to exist until May 1st. I think the
Commanding Officer has definitely given up the idea
of crossing to Greenland, although he has not said so.

Sunday, *March 23rd.*

Rice went down to the shrimp nets at 3 a.m. He
did not get many as one of the net guys broke, up-
setting the net and spilling the contents. At dinner
time he went down again and caught about four
pounds. We could not refrain from giving him a
cheer after this achievement.

As contemplated yesterday I crossed the island to
Rosse Bay. I examined all the bergs and places at
which I thought a seal or walrus likely to appear,
but saw nothing.

We have used the last of our fuel wood. Hence-
forth, as long as the supply holds out, alcohol will
be used for cooking.

March 24th.

Rice made three trips to the shrimping grounds
today, adding to our supplies about seven pounds of
shrimp.

A terrible scene occurred this morning in the hut. While cooking breakfast (tea), the cooks forgot to remove the ventilator from the roof. The fumes from their alcohol lamps soon produced asphyxia. Biederbick was the first to succumb. Israel immediately followed. With one accord the others rushed for the door.

Those who went outdoors were less fortunate than those who fainted inside. As soon as they came in contact with the pure outside air, all strength left them and they fell to the ground in a dead faint. In consequence of the absence of all animation, many of us were frost-bitten.

Through the exertions of Gardiner, the lives of a few were probably saved. With prompt and able attention, Dr. Pavy succeeded in reviving Biederbick and Israel. Gardiner said that I appeared to suffer most and that I fell not less than a dozen times. I would recover, stagger to my feet and immediately faint again. Lieut. Greely, Connell and I were affected more than any of the others.

During the excitement about half a pound of bacon was stolen from Lieut. Greely's mess. When the theft became known there was great indignation in the camp. To think that in our midst was a man with a nature so devoid of humanity as to steal food from his starving companions when they might be dying.

A deed so contemptible and so heartless could not long remain concealed. We were not disappointed in the discovery that Henry was the thief. He had bolted the bacon which was more than his enfeebled stomach could bear. The bacon was quickly ejected before our eyes and Henry's crime revealed. Jens afterward reported having seen Henry commit the theft, going through a pantomime to illustrate his manner of doing it. Threats of lynching were privately made.

March 25th.

A clear, beautiful day. At noon the thermometer exposed in the sun indicated −0.5°. Rice and Whisler went down to the shrimping grounds at 3 p.m. and set a net at the large berg. But a disturbance in the ice removed the baits and few shrimp were obtained. In the evening, though, Rice caught nearly four pounds. Schneider makes the baits by sewing seal skins over large stones. These are placed in the bottom of the net serving as both food and weights to sink the net. The little crustaceans collect on the surfaces of the skins. More than thirteen hundred of them are required to fill a gill measure.

Long and Eskimo Fred went down to the open water, but as usual returned without any game. If we only had a few days of good weather, there might be seals in this pool. One seal would guarantee us another week of life and hope.

Frederik came in greatly exhausted from this trip. He was nearly unconscious and had been half-carried by Long from Cape Sabine. If Long had not been strong enough to assist him this much, Fred would assuredly have perished.

Henry opened his own case this morning by protesting his innocence, but he was confronted with the evidence collected last evening. Jens again illustrated by signs and with his imperfect English, how Henry had accomplished the theft of the bacon. Biederbick and Fredericks told how they had observed that he had eaten none of the rations issued him yesterday morning, and testified to having seen the large quantity of bacon which he vomited into a can last evening.

The testimony of others was added and this alone would have been sufficient to convict him. Long saw him drink two rations of rum issued us yesterday to counteract the effects of our terrible exposure. Ellis now reports him for stealing canned goods at Fort Conger, and Connell related how he had seen Henry under very suspicious circumstances last fall with a new roast beef can in his possession before any of the roast beef had been issued. Rice suggested that Henry be confined closely to the hut as a prisoner and hinted that under the circumstances, violent measures would be in order if the confinement were broken.

Lieut. Greely requested the individual opinion of all and without a single exception we were unanimous in the belief that Henry is guilty and should be punished. He then placed Henry in arrest. He is not to leave his bag without permission, and in no case will he go outdoors unaccompanied.

March 26th.

The English chocolate I found a few days ago and which was being kept for Elison, was missing this morning. Circumstances point strongly to Henry as the guilty party.

In violation of orders, Ellis was discovered today smoking the roots of saxifrage.

Shrimps combined with tallow make an excellent stew.

March 27th.

Lieut. Greely today celebrates the fortieth anniversary of his birth.

Long and Jens went out to open water this morning accompanied by Salor who carried the kayak. The latter returned in about two hours with fifteen dovekies which Long had shot. Lieut. Kislingbury and Connell immediately went out with more ammunition and soon brought in eight more birds. Long was the hero of the hour and the proudest moment of his life was probably when he threw those birds at the feet of Lieut. Greely as a birthday offering. Cheer after cheer was given the hunters and general good feeling prevailed on all sides.

Each dovekie is equal to about one pound of meat. This, I think, is the turning point in our fortunes. Everyone is of the same opinion. Rice had a good day catching twelve pounds of shrimp.

Henry asked Lieut. Greely to be allowed to perform some share of the daily duty in the hut and said, "You will kill me with injustice, if you do not." Crocodile tears to create sympathy came at his bidding, and flowed freely from the eyes which a few days ago looked on the wretched condition of his companions without remorse or pity. His request was received in silence and entirely ignored.

Frederik volunteered to go out to the open water with Long tomorrow, but when refused owing to his enfeebled condition, he cursed in broken English and worked himself into a towering passion.

Lieut. Greely has decided to allow Rice and Fredericks who have volunteered, to start about April 8th to bring in the meat abandoned last fall at Baird Inlet.

Israel tells me he detected the Doctor stealing bread from Elison's can yesterday.

March 28th.

Long shot fourteen dovekies. Rice captured twenty-seven pounds of shrimps. Eskimo Fred shot a ptarmigan on Cemetery Ridge, and returned to the hut immediately much exhausted from the exertion. He seems very despondent and says that he will never return to his home in Proven. Perhaps, he is right.

The evening readings which have been a source of so much gratification were discontinued this evening, owing to an inclination on the part of some to sleep rather than hear them.

March 29th.

Breakfast consisted of four and a half ounces of bread, one ounce bacon, six ounces shrimps and no tea. For dinner we had one and a third ounces of dovekie, one ounce bacon, two and a half ounces bread and eleven ounces shrimps to each man. This made a delightful stew. The solid content was more than we had been accustomed to eat for both meals. Although this makes only two full meals, we are already beginning to note a change in our condition.

Rice shot a ptarmigan and saw five more on the hill near Cemetery Ridge. He caught twelve pounds of shrimp.

Lieut. Greely says he will send me in charge of a party to explore Hayes Sound during May, if we are successful in procuring game.

Poor suffering Elison! This morning turning to the Doctor he said, "My toes are burning dreadfully and the soles of my feet itch. Can't you do something for me?" He has neither toes nor feet. They dropped off early in January, but he has been kept in ignorance of the fact. . . .

March 31st.

A gale has been blowing for three days. There was a lull about noon, but it seemed to gain fresh strength by the short respite and once more began blowing with redoubled fury.

Eskimo Fred complained of feeling faint and he was given a drink of rum. This seemed to restore him, but I am afraid the restoration is only temporary. Sergeant Fredericks was too ill to cook supper. Schneider volunteered to perform the duty for him. The stew was thin and unsatisfactory.

Temperature inside the house this morning was 18°—the lowest recorded since the house was banked last fall. We have been very unsociable and unpleasant toward one another today because, I suppose, of the disagreeable weather.

April 1st.

The gale subsided at 4 a.m.

Rice made four trips to the shrimping grounds, returning with thirty pounds of shrimps. Long killed eleven dovekies and saw four seals, one of which he shot at but did not hit.

This is one of the worst days I have passed in this place. I am so weak from our long fast that I can do little better than reel along alike a drunken man. With the utmost difficulty I persuade myself to move at all. Even the moral power appears to resist the employment of physical energies. Our pinched faces and hollow, lusterless eyes are turned wishfully toward the southern horizon in hope of succor. Will it ever come to us?

III

DEATH

April 2nd.

Rice and Fredericks remained at the fishing grounds seven hours, returning with thirty-two pounds of shrimps.

Eskimo Fred's ration has been increased to the same amount received by the hunters. Fred does not improve. ·In fact, he is failing rapidly. He is now sulky and angry because he is not given more food. He has always been so faithful and devoted that I cannot complain of him now when it is hunger and not the man who speaks. . . .

April 5th.

Eskimo Fred died at 9 a.m. Although not altogether unexpected, his death was very sudden. He was outdoors during the night and ate his breakfast only two hours before he died. He then passed away quietly and without pain. The exposure incident to his trip with Long to Mount Carey last month is the immediate cause of Fred's death. Really, though, he slowly starved to death. His remains were interred on Cemetery Ridge at 2 p.m. and a salute fired over his grave.

Jens did not display the stoicism usually attributed to the people of his race, but exhibited signs of deep and heart-felt emotion. Nevertheless, Jens speaks hopefully of the future and recommends Eskimo Point as an excellent hunting ground. To keep up his spirit at this time when his countryman has passed away, the Commanding Officer has ordered double rations for Jens until further orders.

No game was seen by the hunters today.

I worked nearly all day getting Rice and Fredericks ready for the field. They start for Baird Inlet tomorrow.

I am afraid that Lieut. Lockwood and Linn will soon follow the faithful Eskimo who has just died. They cannot, or will not, eat the shrimps any longer. Although they are given an extra allowance of dovekie, it is not sufficient to restore their depleted strength. Heaven help them!

SUNDAY, *April 6th.*

Linn, our comrade and trusted friend, passed away quietly at 7 p.m. During the winter Linn had been rather petulant and irritable. This was not his natural disposition. His mind was weakened during those awful two days and nights that he and Fredericks spent in the sleeping bag with Elison.

Whatever irritation Linn exhibited, it was quickly forgiven and forgotten by all of us. At Fort Conger in good health he was a noble, generous-hearted, faithful fellow and this is how we always will remember him.

Death in our midst has ceased to rouse our emotions. How indifferently we look on anything of this kind now! After Linn's death, Rice and Ralston slept soundly in the same bag with the corpse which we hope to have strength enough to prepare for burial tomorrow.

As contemplated, Rice and Fredericks departed on their hazardous mission to Baird Inlet at 9:15 p.m. Earlier in the day Lieut. Kislingbury, Ellis and I hauled their travelling equipment on the small sledge to the summit of the island, thus saving their strength somewhat. I do not believe that anyone has ever until today really appreciated the full extent of our weakness. We had to ascend the glacier near the shrimping grounds. Four hours and ten minutes were required to reach the summit and one hour and thirty minutes to return. This trial has fully convinced us of the utter hopelessness of escape to Littleton Island.

Our farewells to Rice and Fredericks were uttered with husky voices and tremulous lips. The silent prayers of those who remained went with them and eyes, to which tears were strangers, were dimmed with the love and fear we felt for these two brave souls. Weak and despondent, they go out alone in the bleak wastes of an Arctic desert, taking their lives in their hands, to bring food to their starving companions. Before them lie famine, indescribable cold, torture to their minds and then, perhaps, failure. And in the hut we must wait for the end of the story.

April 7th.

Snow has been falling heavily all day. Temperature at 6 a.m. —8.7°.

Poor Linn was buried at 10 a.m. Lieut. Kislingbury scooped out a grave for him on Cemetery Ridge which was only six inches deep. It was all eight of us could do to haul the body to the ridge on the large sledge, although Linn was literally a skeleton.

I shot two ptarmigan this morning with one shot.

Biederbick diluted a quantity of alcohol and, with some slight flavoring, made an excellent moonshine drink which imparted warmth and life to the poor fellows for a short time.

Lieut. Lockwood and Jewell will soon follow Linn. They are very weak. Jens is in good spirits and continues to predict success to the hunters with warm weather.

Several of the party are writing their wills, as well as letters to their friends.

April 8th.

All last night and throughout the day, snow has fallen and high winds prevailed. The drift was at times terrific. Rice and Fredericks must be suffering greatly in this storm.

Diluted alcohol was again issued with most satisfactory effect.

Salor said that he was no longer able to walk to

the shrimping grounds, and I have relieved him.
After dinner I went down through the howling storm
and returned at 9 p.m. with 15 pounds of shrimps.

April 9th.

Lieut. Lockwood became unconscious early this
morning and at 4:20 p.m. breathed his last. This
will be a sad blow to his family who evidently
idolize him. To me it is also a sorrowful event. He
had been my companion during long and eventful
excursions, and my feeling toward him was akin
to that of a brother. Biederbick and myself
straightened his limbs and prepared his remains for
burial. This was the saddest duty I have ever yet
been called upon to perform.

Moonshine was again issued today.

The order of August, 1881, relieving Lieut. Kislingbury from duty with the expedition, was revoked
today and that officer once more restored to duty.
Lieut. Greely eulogized him in the highest terms for
his efficient assistance in the retreat from Fort Conger, and expressed a wish that their future inter-
course might be of the most agreeable nature. The
reinstatement was made to provide a second in command, since Lieut. Lockwood is dead.

Ellis was again detected eating stearine and, as a punishment, his dinner was denied him. He wept and begged in the most abject manner for a remission of his sentence, and Lieut. Greely finally modified it so that only half a cup of tea was taken from him.

I took an inventory of provisions this morning with the following result: Meat of all kinds, 156 pounds; bread, 70 pounds. And on this we expect to prolong life another month until May 10th. The future is dark and gloomy. I think that Arctic clouds are seldom seen with a silver lining.

April 10th.

The storm which has been raging for four days, abated about 8 p.m. What can have been the fate of Rice and Fredericks in the snow and wind? I have thought of them every moment, of what they must be suffering and wondered whether they could endure and survive.

Jewell is endeavoring to rally, but the attempt is a feeble one. He does not relish the shrimps and his death by starvation seems inevitable.

The last, sad rites were performed over the remains of Lockwood, and he was interred with the others on Cemetery Ridge.

Although Biederbick is quite ill, he continues in wonderful spirits and does all in his power to cheer his more despondent companions. Gardiner is gradually drooping, and Connell and Ellis are beginning to feel to a marked degree the effects of this horrible life.

Whisler made a most startling statement to both the Commanding Officer and myself, regarding the disloyal conduct of Dr. Pavy during the autumn of 1881, when they were travelling toward Cape Joseph Henry.

[The original diary does not give the particulars of Whisler's statement. Some years later General Brainard inserted the following between the pages of the manuscript:

Fort Bidewell, Cal.,
February 3rd, 1890.

The "disloyal conduct" as stated by Whisler, was to this effect. In October 1881, he [Dr. Pavy] left Fort Conger with party of Private Whisler and Jens, Eskimo dog driver, taking a dog team and sledge with provisions for a journey to Cape Joseph Henry. While on this journey, Whisler states that Dr. Pavy tried to induce him to join in an expedition to the

north the following year, with the intention of making
the highest latitude ever attained, and, further, that
Whisler should join him in stealing the only remaining dog team at the station so that the North Greenland Party [Lieutenant Lockwood and Sergeant
Brainard] could not travel so far, while the Doctor's
party would be enabled to go much farther north.
Whisler says that on his refusal to aid the Doctor in
such a scheme, the latter became angry and abusive,
whereupon W. drew a revolver.

D.L.B.]

Jens is feeling far from well. What could we do
without his assistance?

The alcoholic drink was again issued and pleasant
results followed. I used the last of the bird skins
for shrimp bait this evening.

April 11th.

The most beautiful day that we have had this
month. Clear and a temperature of −23° at 4 a.m.
and the sun shining all day. What more could we
ask?

Long and Jens went down to the open water, but
saw nothing except a walrus, which they could not

reach. Long narrowly escaped being carried away this morning. A piece of the floe on which he was standing at the water's edge, broke from the main body of ice and drifted out to sea. From a distance Jens saw Long's situation and paddled out to him in his kayak. Long urged him in vain to return to the fast ice and save himself. The faithful fellow refused to obey and explained in his simple way, "You go, me go too." Fortunately the turning tide wafted them back to the fast ice.

Israel broke down completely this morning. Jewell does not rally, except under the influence of stimulants. Late in the evening he became delirious.

Owing to my heavy duties, Lieut. Greely ordered me to issue myself two ounces of pemmican daily. He also directed that the rations of Jewell and Israel be increased four ounces each daily. We are all once more at work making imaginary bills of fare, and partaking of sumptuous repasts.

Whisler volunteered to relieve me at the shrimp fishery this morning. He went down at four o'clock, having fished three hours, I brought in about eight pounds. After dinner I went down again. While returning with about three pounds. At 11:30 a.m., waiting for the tardy little crustaceans to collect, I walked up and down to keep from freezing, my mind occupied with thoughts of our deplorable situation and then again with food I would like to have.

Chancing to glance in the direction of Beebe Point, I saw a medium sized bear about two hundred yards away approaching at a shambling gait. My first impulse was to hide behind a hummock and attack with the hatchet and seaweed spear. These, however, did not strike me as particularly devastating weapons for an encounter with a hungry bear, especially when wielded by one whose strength scarcely equals that of a child's. Taking the five pounds of shrimps which I had collected (I could not afford to lose both the shrimps and the bear), I moved away as quickly as I could toward the hut. It seemed ages while I was crawling over Cemetery Ridge. I feared the bear might get away before I could reach the hunters and I feared, too, that he might overtake me. Near the house I abandoned my heavy mittens and shrimp bucket to increase my speed.

Crawling on my hands and knees, I pushed open the door with my head and fell into the hut, yelling, "Bear!!!"

I was too exhausted to say more. A quantity of diluted alcohol was poured down my throat and then in a moment I was able to tell Long and Jens where I had met the bear. They started out immediately. Lieut. Kislingbury also went out but, having run to Cemetery Ridge, he broke down.

At 9:50 p.m. we heard the hunters returning. From the time we heard their footsteps until they entered the hut, the suspense was terrible. Our lives were hanging in the balance and the chances for life or death were equal. And then they came and announced their success. The bear was lying dead within a few feet of the open water about three miles away.

Everything was at once excitement and animation. Within twenty minutes the large sledge was ready and Dr. Pavy, Long, Schneider, Henry, Whisler, Ralston, Salor, Ellis and myself went down to the open water. Before starting three ounces of bacon were issued each that our strength might be maintained.

The open water was reached at midnight and with considerable difficulty the heavy animal loaded and fastened to the sledge. The blood which had flowed from the bullet holes over the ice was chopped out with a hatchet and saved.

This is Good Friday. We hope it is the last fast day we will experience in these regions.

April 12th.

We started back from the open water after midnight, reaching the hut at 2:20 a.m. We had made a most remarkable trip, considering our weak condition. Ellis accompanied us half a mile when his strength was exhausted and he turned back.

Amid feeble cheers, our still more feeble men hauled the glorious prize into the middle of the hut where he was skinned and dressed by Bender and Biederbick. Everything will be utilized—intestines, lungs, heart, head, etc. The liver, wind-pipe, feet and stomach (which was nearly empty) have been set aside for shrimp bait. The blood will thicken our stews.

This fellow is our salvation. Without him Ellis, Connell, Bender, Biederbick, Israel, Gardiner, Salor and Kislingbury would have been in their graves in two weeks. No words can express the rejoicing in our little party today. For days and weeks we had been expecting death at any time, and its approach had been robbed of all its terrors by our sufferings. Life had seemed to us a vague something in the misty distance which was beyond our power to reach or control. Now, to believe that we will be enabled to reach our homes, was sufficient cause for tears.

Jewell died at 10 a.m. without a struggle. Biederbick and myself closed his eyes and straightened his thin limbs. At 2 p.m. he was placed beside the others on Cemetery Ridge. Poor fellow! Had the bear been killed twenty-four hours earlier, he might have been saved.

Lieut. Greely was kind enough to transfer me to the Signal Corps with the rank of sergeant, subject to the approval of the Hon. Secretary of War.

Meat ration has been increased to eight ounces per day. The hunters and shrimper (Long, Jens and myself) will receive eight ounces extra meat daily. Elison also receives the same.

The hunters rested today and Bender repaired their guns.

SUNDAY, *April 13th.*

After two days of joy over the bear, gloom settled

down over the party today with the arrival of Fredericks who reported the death of our beloved friend and comrade, Rice, at Baird Inlet on April 9th, during the progress of the severe storm. They had reached Eskimo Point where they abandoned everything except their sledge, rum, fuel and a few rations. They then proceeded out on the floe of the inlet in search of the meat. No trace of it could be found during the driving storm. Rice at last (3 p.m.) broke down from exhaustion and weakness and at 7:45 p.m. breathed his last. With cheering words and stimulants, Fredericks tried to revive him, but all in vain.

Can anyone conceive a sadder picture than the distracted survivor lying on the sledge with his dead companion in his arms, miles from any human being, and no power on earth to assist him? The storm howled about Fredericks and blinding drift added to his sufferings. He scooped a shallow grave in the snow and in it placed the body of his friend. A heap of broken ice is all that marks the resting place of the bravest and noblest member of this expedition.

Fredericks brought back all their effects on the sledge as far as Cocked Hat Island where he abandoned them. He performed his duty nobly and this trip in which he and Rice participated will ever be conspicuous as one of the most heroic efforts made by men in these regions. Although utterly worn out and weakened by his various trials, Fredericks brought back untouched Rice's remaining rations to be returned to the common larder.

Long shot a small seal at noon and Whisler and I hauled him in. He will weigh about sixty pounds, in addition to twenty-five pounds of blubber.

Lieut. Greely increased our meat ration to one pound daily to offset the sad news of Rice's death and our disappointment in losing the English meat.

Elison was promoted and transferred to the Signal Corps to fill the vacancy left by Rice.

[In the files of the War Department, written in his own hand, is Sergeant Fredericks's report of the death of the "bravest and noblest of this expedition":

"I discovered about 4 p.m. that Rice was weakening. I therefore reminded him of the agreement made before leaving Camp Clay, that in case either of us should show signs of exhaustion his comrade should tell him, in order that necessary steps might be taken to prevent disaster, and I again urged upon Rice the necessity of returning to the sleeping bag for rest and shelter.

"But he said that he was only a little tired, and would soon recover by traveling a little slow. After a short time, however, I could plainly see that Rice was weakening rapidly, and observing an iceberg about 1,000 yards to the west of us, I urged upon Rice to reach it in order to obtain at least a partial shelter. We fortunately accomplished this. By this time he was almost completely exhausted. I gave him some brandy and spirits of ammonia, which seemed to revive him. I now lighted the lamp and prepared some warm food for him; after having eaten it and drunk a cup of warm tea I endeavored to start him, in order to keep him from freezing, but it was all in vain. His condition was becoming alarming. He was too weak to stand up, and his mind seemed to be taken up with recollections of his relatives and friends at home, of whom he spoke, and he also kept talking of the different meals he would eat when he should have reached home. . . . We remained here on this desolate piece of ice, with the wind blowing a hurricane, for two hours, or more, after which time

my poor heroic companion lost consciousness.
I wrapped him up in my *temiak* in order to keep him
as warm as possible, and remained on the sledge
amidst the drifting snow with my unconscious friend
in my arms until 7:45 p.m., when poor Rice passed
away. My situation can be easier imagined than described. Here I was left alone with the body of my
friend in an icebound region, out of reach of help or
assistance. The death of my companion under these
circumstances made a deeper impression on my mind
than any experience in my whole life. As here I
stood, completely exhausted, by the remains of poor
Rice, shivering with the cold, unable to bury the remains, hardly able to move, I knew that my chances
to reach Eskimo Point, which was about 7 miles to
the north, were small indeed. I was completely disheartened; I felt more like remaining here and perishing by the side of my companion than to make another
effort, but the sense of the duty which I owed to my
country and my companions and to my dead comrade
to bear back the sad tidings of the disaster, sustained
me in this trial. I stooped and kissed the remains of
my dead companion and left them there for the wild
winds of the Arctic to sweep over.

"I traveled to the north, and after 7 hours of hard travel I reached the sleeping bag completely exhausted. I found the bag frozen stiff as a piece of cordwood, and in my weak condition I was unable to unroll it, and I thought surely that I should have to perish here; but, as fortune would have it, I found in my pocket a small vial which contained a few drops of ammonia, which I took. This revived me so that it enabled me to get into the bag, where I lay until the following morning. I then hustled out about 8 a.m.; got some warm food, and started back to bury the remains of my companion. . . . When I reached the gloomy spot where lay the remains of poor Rice, thinking that he might have something on his person which ought to be returned to his relatives, I searched his clothing, and found several small articles. . . .

"I then began the difficult task of digging a grave for the remains of my poor friend, which was accomplished after hard labor of several hours. I had no shovel, only an ax, and the loose ice I had to remove with my hands, and it is here, on a paleocrystic floe, that I laid the remains of one who was so dear to me. Here, in this icy grave, I leave my comrade, and will endeavor to carry back the sad news to our

companions. After a few hours I again reached Eskimo Point where I camped for the night. . . ."]

April 14th.

In a letter given to Lieut. Kislingbury before his
departure, Rice appoints M. P. Rice of Washington,
D.C., Lieut. Kislingbury and myself as his executors,
giving explicit directions for the disposition of his
property.

Fredericks has slept nearly all day.

The Commanding Officer has not been feeling well
for the last few days. The Doctor says that he is
suffering from irritation of the heart. In view of the
fact that all who are greatly reduced are receiving
extra rations, Lieut. Greely issued himself a few extra
ounces of bread and pemmican this evening. He has
improved already. By official letter today, Lieut.
Greely appointed me his legal successor in command
of the expedition, in the event of his death, Lieut.
Kislingbury being too ill and feeble to assume the
responsibility.

April 15th.

I caught fifteen pounds of shrimps. Schneider

came down and carried up my can. His assistance was welcome, as I am very weak, having worked too hard the last few days.

Fredericks and Whisler went up to Cocked Hat Island and brought in the sledge and effects which the former had abandoned there a few days ago.

Elison's bread has been reduced to four ounces; the general ration has been reduced to two ounces per day. The issue of diluted alcohol will be continued daily until further orders.

Lieut. Kislingbury and Ellis are quite ill from over-exertion during the bear excitement on the 11 inst. Gardiner fainted this morning, but this evening he feels much better. Lieut. Greely has been ill all day and feeling much weaker than usual, he directed a small extra issue of bread and pemmican for himself.

April 16th.

This morning I caught 18 pounds of shrimps. In the evening, I again hauled the nets which resulted in 23 pounds more. From now on I will leave the nets down and haul them during the low tides twice each day. By this means I will avoid seven hours exposure which has been diminishing what little strength remains to me.

Israel is weaker. His ration has been increased eight ounces. Lieut. Greely has been feeling somewhat better today. He again ate a few ounces of bread and pemmican in the commissary storehouse while I was issuing the provisions. Lieut. Kislingbury and Ellis are in a very weak state.

Our bear meat was fried instead of stewed for the evening meal and the change was an improvement. Ralston was relieved as cook in Lieut. Greely's mess and Fredericks replaced him.

Henry has been parolled and given the limits of the peninsula.

April 17th.

I overhauled the effects of Rice and Jewell, placing them in shape for transportation to their friends.

Fredericks hauled the nets at both tides, securing 42 pounds of shrimps. I returned home last evening exhausted, and today I am scarcely able to move about. Almost everyone is feeling better since the return of the glorious sunlight. Lieut. Greely, especially, has improved during the last few days.

April 18th.

A terrific snow and wind storm raged all day.

Jens is manufacturing a small sledge to support a screen which he will use to hunt seals.

The melting frost from the roof is making us very wretched. Our bags are covered with ice and our clothing cold with moisture.

I am feeling very weak and without ambition.

Whisler appears to be failing rapidly and converses but little.

April 19th.

Members of the expedition are of the opinion that Lieut. Greely's strength should be maintained and, after being urged to do so, he again directed that a small extra issue of pemmican be made him.

Ellis is worse, much worse. He could not eat his breakfast of shrimps. Whisler gave out today. He says that he can do nothing more.

The greatest difficulty I have to contend with in my duties about camp is the issue of fresh meat which frozen firmly, has to be cut with a hand saw. I am too weak for even this simple task. I often feel like giving up.

SUNDAY, *April 20th.*

A breakfast of hard bread and tallow was relished, but the dinner was the event of the entire winter— trimmings of bear and seal heads, their hearts, lungs, kidneys, etc., and a large quantity of bear blood which we had chopped from the ice. The blood enriched the stew beyond conception, making the gravy thick and delicious and imparting a delicacy of flavor.

Dr. Pavy reported to Lieut. Greely that the meat (extra) issued to the hunters was almost wholly without bone. Think of the absurdity of issuing bones to men who are striving with all their might to put food in our mouths!

From this date the midnight sun can be seen from Camp Clay.

April 21st.

Long was the only man strong enough to do the outside work today. He is a wonderful fellow and is doing all in his power to help those who cannot help themselves. Lieut. Greely is recovering slowly.

Schneider accused of some irregularity in the distribution of food to those in the mess for which he is cook, was taken to task by Lieut. Greely. He was given to understand that a repetition of this offense would be a signal for severe measures.

Jens, the happy good-natured, little fellow, is in excellent spirits and full of hope for the future, and says, "Me all same white man."

April 22nd.

Bender and Whisler tore out the lining of the boat which is to be used for fuel. We burned the last of the stearine this evening.

The shrimps had stripped the nets completely of bait, and I caught only six pounds. Tomorrow I intend to work the evening tide.

Dr. Pavy and Lieut. Kislingbury recommended that our ration be increased from 10 ounces to 16 ounces daily. Lieut. Greely objected, but compromised on 12 ounces. We have at this rate provisions for 20 days more.

On Dr. Pavy's recommendation my extra eight ounces of meat were cut off. Several of my comrades offered to turn over to me portions of their ration, to make the amount good so as to enable me to continue shrimping. This, of course, I could not accept. The Doctor desires that all who are strong enough will take turns at fishing. By removing my extra meat, eight ounces daily will be saved.

Lieut. Greely has been feeling far from well, and ordered another slight increase of his ration today.

I issued the contents of the stomach of the seal which was shot recently. This perhaps would be rather trying diet for persons with fastidious tastes, but we would be happy to have all of this that we could eat.

We have discarded reading at present owing to the scarcity of light and lack of interest. Our conversation flags for want of subjects, and all are asleep by 7 p.m. Undoubtedly it is better for us that our troubles are drowned in sleep so that the full extent of our misery may not at all times be apparent.

Lieut. Greely gave me directions today for the disposition of his effects in the event of his death. I also asked as a favor that my effects might be used according to written instructions in my note book.

I advised the increase of the hunters' rations to 24 ounces, but this did not meet with approval. The stomach of the seal issued today consisted of masticated fish. Its flavor resembled the well-known codfish hash of St. John's, N.F.

April 23rd.

A bright, clear and beautiful day with a light, westerly wind. Temperature at 5 a.m. 5°. In the sun the thermometer indicated 45°.

Whisler made a trap door in the roof [boat] above the cooking apparatus. The opening let into the hut the first light in six months. Bender manufactured a stove in which wood can be burned, the old one having become disabled.

The meat ration of Israel and Gardiner was increased four ounces each.

Long and Jens did not see any game today. I sunk the nets before dinner and in the evening hauled 30 pounds of shrimps. I staggered over to the point of land west of camp in search of game, but found nothing—not even a track.

This life is horrible! I am afraid that we will yet all go mad. What keeps us up? One would suppose that an existence not half so miserable as this would be sufficient to drive one to insanity or suicide. In my case, the thoughts of home, the many enjoyments of life and a feeling of responsibility for the poor fellows who look to me to provide food, do more to inspire me to work and to fight to the end.

April 24th.

Dr. Pavy went down at 4 a.m. and put in the nets for the shrimps. I went down after breakfast and found that he had fastened the ropes so that, as the tide rose, the nets were lifted and held suspended. Since the shrimps will only attack the bait unless it rests on the bottom, nothing was found in the nets. He had also filled the nets with rocks and discarded the baits. When asked why, he replied, "I was thinking of something else."

Schneider made a trip to the nets at 1 p.m., and did fairly well, returning with eight pounds. He lost two pounds by falling down, and he also lost my large ladle with which I remove the shrimps from the net. At five o'clock, I made a trip returning at 7:30 p.m. with 12 pounds. Long and Jens saw an oo-sook seal, but were not near enough to him to get a shot.

Israel and Gardiner, poor fellows, with characteristic unselfishness, did not wish to take the extra four ounces of meat ordered for them, but wanted it turned over to me that my strength may be maintained while acting as shrimper.

Lieuts. Greely and Kislingbury are feeling much worse than usual.

April 25th.

Stormy and disagreeable.

Schneider caught 10 pounds of shrimps this morning. He has had to give up, though, and can do nothing more for the party. Visiting the fishery soon after Schneider, I found that he had left the nets suspended midway between the bottom and the ice. Consequently I secured only a few stragglers. I went down again at 6 p.m. and landed 16 pounds.

My legs are very weak, sore and swollen. The eight extra ounces of meat ordered discontinued a few days ago have been given me again by Lieut. Greely. I shall endeavor to make three trips daily for shrimps. I shot two ptarmigans on Cemetery Ridge.

By actual count seven hundred shrimps weigh an ounce. They possess little nutriment; about three-fourths is shell and one-fourth meat. . . .

SUNDAY, *April 27th.*

The ration of the hunters has been increased four ounces each. They went out at an early hour this morning and did not return until late. Twelve white whales were seen and Jens shot a seal, but without effect. When they returned, the faithful Jens said in his honest way, "Eskimo, no good."

Henry made the issue of diluted alcohol today without authority, stealing enough of the precious fluid to make himself disgustingly drunk. He is a born thief.

We are struggling bravely for life, how bravely the world will probably never know, as none are likely to live to tell the tale. Words written in this journal are not adequate to describe the horrors of our situation. At the present time with the exception of the one who is branded with the title of thief, all are doing their best to prolong life and live harmoniously.

A few mornings past Ralston spilled his stew and Schneider his tea. Everyone contributed from his meager portion to make up their losses.

Great indignation was felt over Henry's theft. Gardiner crawled on his hands and knees (too weak to walk) to reach Henry, with every intention of throttling him.

April 28th.

My tour at the fishery from 5 a.m. to 9:30 resulted

in 25 pounds of shrimps. I also caught considerable marine vegetation with the long pole. Fredericks went down in the evening and brought back 10 pounds of shrimps. The morning fishing left me so weak that I was not equal to a second trip.

Israel and Biederbick are not as well as yesterday. The latter fainted away this evening owing to an abnormal state of his bowels. The same conditions exist with all, there being a movement on the average once a week.

Jens is in excellent spirits. Lieut. Greely has promised him a new kayak; Israel, a new watch; Lieut. Kislingbury and Biederbick, a boat.

The daily ration of diluted alcohol has been taken from Henry. As a prisoner he is detailed to empty the urinal and to perform other menial duties.

April 29th.

By making two trips to the fishery, I captured thirty pounds of shrimps.

Long returned alone at 2:30 p.m. with the dispiriting report, "Jens is drowned!" He had seen a large seal on a drifting cake of ice. Several lanes of water intervened between him and the animal. In transporting his kayak over the ice, which Jens did by pushing it ahead of him, a hole probably was made through the thin seal skin covering. When he reembarked the water rushed in through the opening and he was soon powerless in its icy coldness. Jens sprang upright and then fell forward without uttering a cry for assistance. His body floated for a few minutes and then sank slowly from sight.

Long nearly lost his life trying to rescue the body of his comrade. He also tried to save the kayak which was drifting bottom up, and the Springfield rifle; but both were lost. This is a sad blow to this party. Without the assistance of the kayak, the seals that may be killed cannot be saved.

Hereafter, Fredericks will hunt during the night and Long during the day.

A terrific, southerly gale began at 7 p.m. It will probably break up the straits again.

Our poor Jens! He had grown very dear to us.

April 30th.

This has been a truly fine day. The gale subsided at 1 a.m. and by nine o'clock, the sky cleared to admit the radiant face of old Sol.

Long is afflicted with snow blindness.

I have constructed a rake of iron barrel hoops with which I made quite a successful haul of seaweed and vegetation at the fishery. If we do not secure more game, it is quite possible that we can eke out a miserable existence on shrimps and this vegetation until the arrival of the birds next month.

Lieut. Greely is feeling better. He told me that a letter would be found in his journal directing me to assume command of the expedition in the event of his death. Lieut. Kislingbury's mind is in such a weak state that he is wholly unfitted to command. In the event of my death, Ralston, Gardiner, Fredericks and Long would take charge in the order named.

Everyone, except Lieut. Kislingbury, appears to be holding his own.

Turf, roots and leaves of saxifrage are now used extensively to supplement our other fuel. This will serve to extend our wood for several days.

Snow began falling at 6 p.m.

May 1st.

Snow has been falling steadily all day.

The last of the lime juice pemmican was used yesterday, except a pound or so kept for an emergency. The remainder of the English pemmican was issued today, and tomorrow the last of our bread will be given out.

Will this last, sad blow—the death of Jens—prove fatal to us? Something tells me it will not, although I can give no reason for such impression.

Provisions for nine days only remain. We can scarcely realize that we are so near our end and all sorts of subjects are daily being discussed. Food, the subject which is nearer the hearts of all than any other, of course, excites the most interest. I think it probable we could live on shrimps and sea vegetation alone if it were possible to secure them in sufficient quantities. My bait for the former is nearly exhausted and my strength is going so fast that to haul the iron rake for the vegetation will be an impossibility in a few days. I cannot supply these articles for eighteen persons for many more days. There is but little nutriment in either article and an immense quantity would be required to maintain life.

I fished for six hours this morning, capturing 23 pounds of shrimps and six pounds of sea vegetation, or kelp as we call it.

Lieut. Kislingbury's mind is almost gone. Only a few days ago he talked so hopefully of the future and the happy meeting with his young sons. Yesterday he threw himself on the small sledge outside and, weeping like a child, he said, "It is hopeless. I cannot fight longer!"

Lieut. Greely asked our individual opinion as to the extension of our provisions beyond the date already agreed on. The majority were in favor of reducing them to the minimum.

May 2nd.

The future does not look promising. We see our doom impending and even look forward to death as a relief from suffering. A member of the party remarked this afternoon, "Our frames are much too thin and weak to make a substantial hat rack."

Our rations have been reduced to eight ounces per man, except for the hunters, the shrimper, Elison and Israel.

May 3rd.

Long went down to Rice Strait in search of game. He did his work thoroughly, returning after an absence of fifteen hours. He shot a small seal in a pool there, but it sank. Fredericks came in at 1 a.m. empty-handed, and went out again at eight o'clock.

I caught 25 pounds of shrimps and six pounds of kelp. I use the bear's liver for bait. During the next spring tides, I expect to get enough kelp to last ten or fifteen days. I shot a brace of ptarmigans on Cemetery Ridge this morning.

Lieut. Greely is quite ill. Talking with me he said, "I think that I am near my end." He has eaten only three or four spoonfuls of stew today.

The saxifrage is doing good work as fuel. A large quantity was gathered by Henry today who is considerably stronger than any of the others. He is still a prisoner.

Temperature at 6 a.m. 0°. Very low for this season of the year. Even Nature is against us.

While I was away this morning, Bender detected Whisler in the storehouse. He had forced the lock and when found was eating ravenously of the bacon. A large piece (about two pounds) was found concealed in the breast of his coat. He is now penitent, but in performing such an act at this critical period, little or no sympathy is felt for him.

Will anyone ever be able to decipher this writing?
It is in great part illegible, the sentences disconnected
and incoherent and written in semi-darkness with
great rapidity.

[Lieutenant Greely comments on Whisler's lapse in
his official report:

". . . Whisler was detected taking about a pound
of bacon from the storehouse, the door of which had
been forced. . . . Whisler claimed that the door
must have been forced by Bender or Henry, as he saw
it open . . . and . . . his terrible hunger overcame
his principles. . . . Private Whisler moreover expressed his willingness to be killed or meet any other
fate the party might award, but deplored his mental
weakness which caused his sinning. I believed the
man's confession and in his deep repentance, which
he manifested to his dying day."]

SUNDAY, *May 4th.*

I caught thirty pounds of shrimps and two of sea
vegetation. I am steadily adding to the natural history collection, which we have been accumulating in
alcohol.

To the relief of all, Lieut. Greely is better today.

May 5th.

Long returned shortly after midnight and reported that he had seen nothing. The hunting tour of Fredericks resulted in the same manner. I caught 28 pounds of shrimps and three pounds of kelp.

Lieut. Greely gave me full and explicit instructions for future action in the event of his death, and sent several verbal messages to his wife, Gen. Hazen and others, all of which I have written down.

Dr. Pavy tells me my strength is failing fast and he detects difficulty with my heart which is due to over-exertion.

May 6th.

A S.E. gale rose at 3:30 a.m. and continued with great violence until 1 p.m. Temperature at 1 p.m. 14°. The tunnel or passage leading into the house was drifted full during the gale and the door completely blocked by snow. The men were feeling wretchedly.

Half a lemon was used to flavor the diluted alcohol this morning. One and a half lemons remain, the only luxury in Ellesmere Land. By his order I issued Lieut. Greely one pound of lime juice pemmican for his use for four days. Four ounces of Elison's extra ration has been discontinued.

I repaired to the fishery after dinner and during three hours work caught 12 pounds of shrimps and two of kelp. A heavy snow storm was in progress at the time.

For a long time the Doctor has been objecting to certain arrangements by Lieut. Greely, particularly to the distribution of provisions. Today he had a stormy discussion with Lieut. Greely, during which the latter repeatedly told him to "shut up." Notwithstanding this order, Dr. Pavy continued on in an abusive way when Lieut. Greely said, "If you were not the Surgeon of this Expedition I would shoot you!"

At this point Bender interfered.

He was also threatened with the dose which had been offered to Pavy a moment before. As Bender continued to talk, Lieut. Greely seized Long's rifle and was about to raise it when I removed it from his hand and made Bender crawl into his sleeping bag. In a few moments everything was as tranquil as before, and we are again earnestly considering an imaginary bill of fare.

May 7th.

Many, including myself, spent the greater portion of the day inditing farewell letters to friends and relatives. I also addressed one to the officer commanding the relief party, which will probably reach us too late, in order that he might find everything of value without loss of time.

Gardiner, Lieut. Kislingbury and Ellis are worse.

A large section was cut from the side of the boat and the opening made was covered with canvas to keep out the drifting snow. The wood will be used for fuel.

At 2:30 p.m. the wind began to blow a gale. I started out at three o'clock to visit the fishery, but had not sufficient strength to face the wind. I was blown off the crest of Cemetery Ridge several times and had finally to crawl on my hands and knees back to the hut.

May 8th.

Wind subsided at 11 a.m. A short time previously snow began to fall heavily. At 2 p.m. it ceased and the sun shone brightly. Temperature at 7 a.m. 16°; at 9 p.m. 6°.

The sound now appears to be entirely open and a vessel could navigate its waters with impunity.

May 9th.

Fredericks returned at 1:30 a.m., having killed nothing. He saw numerous seals and gulls which we might have had if Jens and his kayak had been there.

The Doctor thinks it highly probable we can live a short time on shrimps and vegetation after the last of our provisions have been issued. I do not know how the weaker ones can possibly survive the reduction in provisions in the low state of their systems. Dr. Pavy is doing wonderfully well at present. He cuts all the ice, attends assiduously to the sick, gives lectures and bustles about for the good of all.

Salor and Whisler made their wills today.

May 10th.

Fredericks returned at 2 a.m. without having shot anything. He went out again after dinner. Long had no luck either.

I caught 36 pounds of shrimps and dragged up 10 pounds of vegetation. This required over 6 hours,

I was greatly exhausted and when climbing the ice-foot, blood gushed from my nostrils. I sat down for a few minutes in order to recover from the faintness which had come over me and in short time the blood ceased to flow. The Doctor tells me the hemorrhage was due to over-exertion.

The Greenland coast looms up very plain tonight and Smith Sound, perfectly free of ice, is open to Littleton Island. Long said that standing on the summit of Cape Sabine, he could see no ice north or south as far as his vision extended. This looks favorable for the early arrival of relief ships, or the party which we believe to be at Littleton Island.

SUNDAY, *May 11th.*

A clear, beautiful day with only a suspicion of a light breeze from the west. Temperature at 3 p.m. 7.5°.

Fredericks returned at 2 a.m. He had shot a large seal which sank before it drifted to the margin of the ice where he was. This is a sad loss. He went out again this evening after dinner. Long started out after breakfast returning at 4 p.m. without success.

Newly formed ice in great fields has been crowding down from the north all day, drifting with the current southward.

The remainder of the pemmican was issued this morning; also the last of the fresh meat, except ten pounds which Lieut. Greely ordered me to keep for the present.

Gardiner is slightly better. Lieut. Kislingbury and Ellis are worse.

May 12th.

I issued the last of our provisions today. The issue consisted of twelve and a half ounces of bacon and tallow to each man. This is intended to last for two days, but if they choose it can be consumed at once. In addition one ounce of tallow to each per meal was issued for shrimp stews for six meals. The extra for the hunters and shrimper extends only through to-morrow. Heaven only knows what we will do now. Present indications are that we can do nothing but—die.

Israel is very depressed and has made a verbal will. Death we talk freely of, but it is more a matter of business than dread of its approach.

Another large section of the boat was removed

this morning. This leaves only the short passage next the house.

I caught 25 pounds of shrimps and five pounds of kelp. Fredericks did not go out this evening as a severe storm rose after dinner. Nothing can exceed the unselfish devotion of Long and Fredericks. They go out day after day and tramp about in the cold, wet snow, generally to be disappointed, but always hopeful of the morrow's hunting.

May 13th.

A clear, beautiful day with no wind. Temperature at 10 a.m. 14°. All of us were out to enjoy the warmth of the sun except Elison.

Ellis will probably go in a few days. He fell down in the passage this morning unable to use his limbs. We all stagger when we walk. Long is ill today. Fredericks went out as usual. Schneider had to be relieved from cooking this morning on account of faintness. Henry replaced him.

Some of the men have eaten their two days ration of bacon and will now have to depend on the shrimps. I had Bender construct a dredge from the large tin bacon can with which I endeavored to secure a few mollusks. I made several hauls, but captured nothing but sand.

I caught 22 pounds of shrimps and four pounds of kelp. I carry the shrimps in two large tin buckets slung across my shoulders by a strap. It is very fatiguing. I do not think that my strength can be sustained many more days.

May 14th.

Both the hunters went out this morning, returning at 4 p.m., without having had any luck. Bender has made a screen for their use in approaching game.

Schneider is feeling somewhat better. As a matter of precaution and business he made his will today. Israel was very ill during the morning, but toward evening felt better. Poor fellow! We are all in the same condition with nothing before us, but to die like men and soldiers. Lieuts. Greely and Kislingbury, and Ellis are weaker. During the morning we were all lying outside, basking in the sunshine like seals. The sun appears to add strength to our feeble limbs.

After five hours of hard labor this evening, I caught only two pounds of vegetation and 20 pounds of shrimps. My baits are poor, but I am utilizing every ounce of skin and liver remaining from the bear. Oil-tanned seal skin as bait is of little use.

May 15th.

Long attempted to reach the open water this morning, but was too faint and had to drag himself back to our wretched den. All are weaker. Fredericks returned from hunting at 3 p.m. with the discouraging report that he had seen nothing.

Dr. Pavy informs me that Schneider has symptoms of scurvy.

Our last solid food will be eaten tonight in a stew. This consists of one ounce of tallow to each man. All other stews will contain nothing but shrimps and water.

After six hours I secured only 21 pounds of shrimps and three pounds of kelp. I was badly broken down from the exertion. About four days more of this strain will use me up entirely.

May 16th.

My baits are so riddled that I got only nine pounds today; two pounds of kelp. My strength is scarcely sufficient to drag the heavy rake along the bottom.

I hope that someone can assume my duties when I fail. I have changed to the morning tide on account of the sunlight.

Connell went up the coast to the west on the lookout for game, but returned fatigued and disappointed. The large wall tent was hauled up to Cemetery Ridge and pitched there in readiness to shelter the last survivors. The melting snow has made our hut too wet to remain in longer.

Lieuts. Greely and Kislingbury, Gardiner and Ellis are worse. Salor is too unwell to cook. Schneider appears to be the only one who is improving. Whisler broke down this evening. He was not able to cut wood enough for breakfast. Bender who is coming bravely to the front in this trying period, prepared the wood for him.

Smith Sound today was a rolling, billowy sea, entirely free of drifting ice, and with nothing to hinder small boats crossing from Littleton Island. I am convinced there is no rescue party on the island.

[Sergeant Brainard, of course, was correct. There was no rescue party at Littleton Island. After the *Proteus* disaster Lieutenant Garlington and his party crossed to Littleton Island in two whale-boats with the hope of meeting the *Yantic*, the slow naval vessel which had been trailing them. The *Yantic* had not arrived at the island and Lieutenant Garlington, after his misadventure in the ice, was certain the ship would never succeed in plowing through the ice in Melville Bay. He began a hurried retreat southward to bring aid to the Lady Franklin Bay Expedition before winter set in.

The *Yantic* reached Littleton Island eight days after the Garlington party left. It carried supplies sufficient for the relief party to have wintered on the island. A quick search of the island cairn revealed Lieutenant Garlington's record of the *Proteus* wreck, and then the *Yantic* turned about and steamed southward to overtake the retreating wreck party. She did not overtake them, though, until too late to do any good.

The naval vessel called at the islands and harbors which Lieutenant Garlington before going north in the *Proteus* had specified as possible meeting places, or points at which he would attempt to communicate. Lieutenant Garlington retreated south under the misapprehension that the *Yantic* could not reach the north waters, and, to hasten his retreat, touched at none of the out of the way stations previously agreed upon. Not until September second at Upernivik did he and the *Yantic* at last connect. The season was then too far advanced to send another party north to the relief of Greely.

Thus it was that Lieutenant Garlington blundered and sealed the fate of the Lady Franklin Bay Expedition. If he had only gambled on the one chance that the *Yantic* might pull through! All that was required of him was an order, before he started back south, directing the naval vessel to remain at Littleton Island and establish the promised station.]

May 17th.

A clear, beautiful day. At noon a thermometer exposed in the sun indicated 40°. Every bright day we lie on a pile of old clothing and sleeping bags outside and bask in the sunlight.

I caught 16 pounds of shrimps and four pounds of vegetation. Extremely tired and weak afterward. The hunters and myself receive a double ration of the thin shrimp stew.

A portion of a can of lard, which had been used as ointment for Elison's wounds, was today issued in equal portions to all. The remainder of the diluted alcohol was also issued. The green buds of saxifrage have been introduced by some in their stews. It has not upset their stomachs and appears to be nutritive.

SUNDAY, *May 18th.*

Long shot a large raven at 5 a.m. I had attempted it only two hours earlier, but the bird escaped me. He will be used for shrimp bait. I fished in a storm all forenoon, but caught only ten pounds and about two of vegetation.

A vessel could have sailed in Smith Sound today. It was iceless.

To the joy of all, three more issues of alcohol were found in a rubber bag in the boat.

May 19th.

Fredericks went out at 4 a.m. to cut ice for breakfast. In a moment he returned greatly excited, with the welcome information, "Bear outside." He and Long immediately started in pursuit with their rifles. I followed more leisurely with the shot gun. After an hour's tramp, I turned back, not wishing to break down my strength and compromise the source of our only support—the shrimps.

Fredericks returned at 10 a.m. and Long came in about an hour later. Neither had been able to get within range of the animal. They were thoroughly exhausted by their arduous journey, and had turned back while they had strength enough to reach Camp Clay. When first seen this morning, the bear was standing a few feet from the hut.

The large English sledge was cut up for fuel to-day. Ellis quietly breathed his last at 10:30 a.m. No symptoms of scurvy were apparent. Death was due solely to starvation.

The last issue of diluted alcohol was made today.

May 20th.

Ellis was buried at noon on Cemetery Ridge. We could scarcely find enough men with strength sufficient to haul his remains.

If our government does not send a vessel with the whalers when they pass Melville Bay in the early days of June, it will be an act of criminal negligence, or else inexcusable ignorance.

Today I caught only twelve pounds of shrimps and

two of kelp. Another bear or a large seal would save us all from a fate similar to that which over-took the party under Franklin.

May 21st.

I had a long conversation with Lieut. Greely this morning. He is not at all hopeful. He desires me to take charge of some of his papers and in the event of his death, I am to place them in the hands of the Chief Signal Officer.

Dr. Pavy circulated a paper written by himself, certifying to his medical skill and his devotion to his professional duties, and asked for signers. He did this, of course, to offset the fact of his arrest last autumn when he refused to reenlist. About fourteen of the men signed the paper, but Lieut. Greely either would not, or was not asked.

May 22nd.

The tent was placed in position near Cemetery Ridge. Five of the party will sleep in it tonight.

Ralston is most likely dying now (4 p.m.). He drank some rum two hours ago and during the fore-noon ate large quantities of the saxifrage and sang a song. Less than an hour ago, Lieut. Greely fed him with a portion of his shrimp stew. Now he is delirious.

The meagre amount of food consumed does not require our bowels to function oftener than from twelve to eighteen days. This act is always attended with great pain and followed by extreme exhaustion.

May 23rd.

With the exception of the five strongest, the party has moved to the hill. The tent with a small shelter in front accommodates them all. Elison was moved on his mattress—a wearing task, but without pain or injury to him.

Israel is so weak that he had to be hauled on a sledge. Lieut. Kislingbury and Whisler are about as bad. They cannot long survive.

I caught only ten pounds of shrimps. My strength was not equal to managing the kelp rake. Fredericks has worked faithfully today in erecting the shelter in front of the tent and making the sick comfortable.

Ralston died at 1 a.m. His end appeared painless. His remains were not buried owing to the excessive weakness of our strongest men.

May 24th.

Dr. Pavy, Salor, Long and myself slept in the shanty which had been our winter abode. It is damp and without a roof and pretty well dismantled.

Ralston was buried before breakfast. Whisler died at noon. The Doctor says his death was caused by fright. With nutritious food he would have had no cause to feel frightened. He died begging forgiveness for having stolen some bacon several weeks ago.

I overhauled the effects of our dead comrades and placed them in shape for transportation home.

Schneider's face is quite badly swollen, probably from the effects of eating saxifrage, now used in place of sea vegetation which I am no longer able to obtain.

Caterpillars are getting quite numerous now on the bare spots on Cemetery Ridge. Bender saw one crawling near the tent yesterday and hastily transferred it to his mouth, remarking, "This is too much meat to lose."

SUNDAY, *May 25th.*

Southeasterly wind began blowing at 10 a.m. and

continued all day. In the evening it blew a moderate
gale. In the heavy drift I was unable to make the
customary trip to the shrimping grounds, although
the demand for them is great.

We buried Whisler after dinner when the storm
was at its height.

Four of us still sleep in the old shanty and are
but poorly protected against the storms. But there
is no remedy for the matter. Our strength is not
equal to the task of getting out the canvas necessary
to build a shelter.

My God! This life is horrible; will it never
change?

Seal skin thongs cut into small pieces were used
in the stew this evening to eke out the scanty supply
of shrimps. Small quantities of the skin were burned
to a cinder on the fire and then ravenously devoured.

May 26th.

Schneider was detected stealing food (shrimps and
tea) and was also accused of making unfair divisions
in the issue of these articles. He was relieved from
the duties of cook and Bender has volunteered to do
the cooking for both messes.

For the first time this year, sufficient water for preparing supper was collected from pools among the rocks. With the exception of a few drifting fragments, Smith Sound is free of ice and a vessel can navigate any portion of it with perfect impunity.

I caught eight pounds of shrimps and two of vegetation before breakfast. I could have obtained more under ordinary physical conditions, but owing to excessive weakness and a dull throbbing in my head, I was compelled to desist. In the evening, I went down again and returned at eleven o'clock with 12 pounds more. I will try to extend the few inferior shrimp baits until June 1st. After that date unless we get game, we will have to depend on sea vegetation, saxifrage and a small black lichen (tripe de roche) which grows here on the rocks in abundance.

A few garments of seal skin and boots of the same material, together with our oil-tanned sleeping bag covers, will have to be used as a substitute for meat. The soles from an old pair of seal skin boots furnished us, in addition to a few shrimps, with a scanty breakfast and supper. Long killed two dovekies, but they were drifted away by the tide.

May 27th.

Israel, the youngest member of our party, passed away just after midnight. He died very easily and after losing consciousness which was about eleven hours before his death, he talked of food, restaurants, etc. His frankness, honesty and generosity had won the hearts of all. For lack of strength, we could not bury him today.

We worked nearly all day to erect a shelter in front of the tent, and tonight we will all sleep together. I was too exhausted to fish.

A heated discussion about the medicines took place between Lieut. Greely and Dr. Pavy, the details of which I have neither the interest, the inclination nor the strength to record.

May 28th.

I caught nine pounds of shrimps and Long returned from open water with a dovekie. The dovekie was divided between Long and myself by general acclamation.

The sound is now open and as free of ice as in August 1881, when we steamed northward to Lady Franklin Bay. If there is a rescue party somewhere near, why do they not come while there is yet time to save a few lives?

Israel was buried at noon on Cemetery Ridge.

The invalids are about the same as yesterday.

I shall never forget the delicacy of flavor of the dovekie stew which I ate this evening.

May 29th.

Clear, calm weather in the forenoon, but at 1 p.m. the sky clouded and almost immediately after a southeast gale burst upon us. The drift penetrated our rude shelter, defying all efforts to keep it out. The shelter was first blown full of snow and gravel and then blown down. The poles which supported the canvas are now lying across our bodies. In the tent they are better protected, but still their lot is far from pleasant.

Long was driven from the edge of the ice by the approach of the storm and joining me at the fishery, we returned together; but only after a struggle in the gale. I had caught eight pounds of shrimps and Long had one dovekie. I went to the old hut for wood and while there the storm increased, confining me to its walls for two weary hours. On returning to the tent, the Doctor and Salor refused to admit me to the bag in which I occupied a place and in which they were lying. I had to crawl into one of the abandoned bags outside. This was frozen and drifted full of snow. The gale prevented cooking our scanty supper of shrimps and in consequence we ate nothing.

Although I gave directions yesterday that all scraps and pieces of seal skin were to be considered public property, Bender was detected eating some. He confessed and in explanation said that he could not resist the temptation. I told Fredericks to collect everything eatable in the way of seal skin and I would lock it in the storehouse.

May 30th.

The gale did not abate until after midnight. I passed a wretched night outdoors in the wild fury of the storm. A large snow drift accumulated inside and about my sleeping bag and my hands, feet and face were swollen from exposure. Rheumatic pains seized hold of me and, smarting under the wrong done me by my sleeping bag companions, mental agony was added to physical torture.

Our breakfast of shrimps was eaten at 10 a.m. We had fasted twenty-six hours. Today I caught six pounds of shrimps. The last piece of bait was placed in the nets. It will last a few days more.

How we manage to live on from six to ten pounds of shrimps per day I have no idea. Those who do not work because of weakness retain remarkably well the little strength they have.

A gale from the northwest began at 6 p.m. This is the most uninviting region.

May 31st.

The gale continued all day and was accompanied by a heavy snowstorm. We were not only held close prisoners in our shelter, but also in our bags, as drift over a foot deep covered us. We were unable to cook and consequently had nothing to eat during the day, not even a swallow of water.

Of all the days of suffering, none can compare with this. If I knew I had another month of this existence, I would stop the engine this moment.

In my daily journeys across Cemetery Ridge to the fishery, it was but natural at first that my reflections should be sad and gloomy. There lie my departed comrades and to their left is the vacant space where, in a few days, my remains will be deposited if sufficient strength remains to those who may survive me. The brass buttons on Lieut. Lockwood's blouse, worn bright by the flying gravel, protrude through the scanty covering of earth which our depleted strength barely enabled us to place over him. At first, these dazzling buttons would awaken thoughts of those bright days at Fort Conger and the half-forgotten scene of his death, and the universal sorrow that was felt at his departure. But later, my own wretched circumstances have served to counteract these feelings, and I can pass and repass this place without emotion and almost with indifference.

SUNDAY, *June 1st.*

The gale subsiding at 1 a.m., we immediately turned out of our comfortable quarters to remove the snow which had accumulated over us. The snow had also penetrated our sleeping bags.

Breakfast consisted of three ounces of shrimps and a cup of weak tea to each man. This is a fair sample of our meals at present. We were without food for over thirty-six hours.

Lieut. Kislingbury became unconscious at 8 a.m. and breathed his last at 3 p.m. Before he lost consciousness he begged piteously for a drink of water, but this the Doctor denied him. He then sang the Doxology in a clear but weak voice and, falling back in his sleeping bag, was soon in the embrace of Death.

The sky cleared at 8 a.m. and the sun came out bright and clear. At 3 p.m. the sky again clouded and light snow began falling. Temperature at 10 a.m. 35°.

Pools of water are forming everywhere in the rocks and in depressions about our tent. Water sufficient for two days was collected by the cooks. It is very fortunate as our fuel is fast disappearing.

Long shot a dovekie. One of his eyes was injured by the recoil of his gun and I had to lead him home.

I caught eight pounds of shrimps. The snow is very deep and soft. Long and I were gone from the house over seven hours. Less than two hours were spent at the fishery, the remainder of the time being consumed in walking. We felt ready to drop from fatigue on returning. My knees are stiff and swollen and I cannot bend them.

June 2nd.

After an absence of over seven hours, I returned with only five pounds of shrimps. My baits are almost useless.

We buried Lieut. Kislingbury this morning.

Schneider is no longer able to work. Bender is little better. Lieut. Greely and Gardiner are very weak. Salor became delirious at 7 p.m.

Long shot a dovekie.

Vast fields of ice are moving down the sound. If it would choke in the narrow part, this might drive the seals and birds to this side.

June 3rd.

Fair weather. A light wind blew steadily from the southeast all day and thawing advanced considerably. Water is trickling down the hillside, forming in pools near the tent and thus providing all the water required.

Long did not go out today owing to windy weather.

I caught only six pounds of shrimps.

Salor died at 3 a.m. I was lying by his side in the same bag at the time. Not having the necessary strength to remove him and not feeling inclined to get up, I went to sleep in the same bag with his remains and did not awake until breakfast was announced at 9 a.m.

Doctor Pavy was making some rather absurd prescriptions this evening and talking incoherently.

For weeks I have noticed Linn's feet protruding from the gravel heaped over his body. Day by day the elements have reduced the scanty covering until Linn's feet are fully exposed to the gales sweeping over Cemetery Ridge. I have often thought that I would replace that which had blown away, but my waning strength has caused me to defer this for so long that I cannot think of attempting it now.

June 4th.

A beautiful day. The wind which was blowing last evening abated at 6 a.m., but again sprang up this evening. High, blustering wind storms appear to be normal weather here.

I caught seven pounds of shrimps and Long shot a dovekie.

Fredericks, occasionally assisted by Henry, is doing all the work about camp—cooking, gathering saxifrage for fuel, and cutting wood from the boat.

Schneider manages to bring in salt water for the cook, but can do nothing more. Bender and Connell can do but very little.

During the last few days, I have eaten a great many of the dark colored rock lichens, finding them quite palatable and not at all injurious to the stomach, the experiences of Franklin and Hayes notwithstanding. Lieut. Greely is of the opinion that they contain some nutriment.

Smith Sound is a beautiful sheet of water today, not a piece of ice in sight and the surface as smooth as a mirror. How easily we could be reached by a relief vessel or a party from Littleton Island!

We buried Salor in the tidal crack. We did not feel strong enough to dig a grave on Cemetery Ridge.

June 5th.

Dr. Pavy is very weak. He refuses to partake of the shrimp stew and is kept up by weak tea alone.

I caught five pounds of shrimps.

Reindeer moss in small quantities has been found at this point. The vegetation—poppies, saxifrage, grasses, etc.—is becoming green. The mosses growing in damp ground are looking quite beautiful.

Owing to the thievish propensity of Henry which has again broken out, it became necessary in order to insure the safety of the party for Lieut. Greely to issue an order to Long, Fredericks and myself to shoot him without delay, if detected in appropriating to his own use any articles of public property. I insert a copy of the order.

> Near Cape Sabine,
> June 5th, 1884.

To Sergeants Brainard, Fredericks and Long:

Private Henry having been repeatedly guilty of stealing the provisions of this party which is now perishing slowly by starvation, has so far been condoned and pardoned. It is, however, *imperatively ordered* that if this man be detected either eating food of any kind not issued him regularly, or making caches, or appropriating any article of provisions, you will at once shoot him and report the matter to me. Any other course would be a fatal leniency, the man being able to overpower any two of our present force.

> (signed) A. W. Greely,
> Lt. 5th Cav. A. S. O. & Asst.
> Comdg. Lady Franklin Bay Ex.

Henry has twice stolen the greater portion of dovekie intended for the hunter and the shrimper. He was also detected eating seal skin lashing and seal skin boots stolen from the public stock. The stealing of old seal skin boots etc. may seem to some a very insignificant affair, but to us such articles mean life.

June 6th.

I fished over seven hours for the tantalizing little shrimps and caught only two and a half pounds. My baits are almost worthless. What are we to do? I have tried everything at hand, but with no favorable results. I would again drag for sea vegetation, but my failing strength is not equal to the task. I can do nothing more than stagger down to the shrimping grounds and return.

A further confession on the part of Henry to Lieut. Greely of stealing and the fact of his having been caught stealing shrimps this morning, caused the issuing of the following order:

Near Cape Sabine,
June 6th, 1884.
Sergeants Brainard, Long and Fredericks:
Notwithstanding promises given by Private C. B.

Henry yesterday he has since acknowledged to me having tampered with seal thongs, if not other food at the old camp. This pertinacity and audacity is the destruction of this party if not at once ended. Private Henry will be shot today, all care being taken to prevent his injuring anyone as his physical strength is greater than that of any two men. Decide the manner of death by two ball and one blank cartridge.

This order is *imperative* and *absolutely necessary* for *any chance* of life.

(Signed) A. W. Greely,

1st. Lt. 5th Cav. A. S. O. & Asst.

Comdg. L. F. B. Ex.

No further explanation in the matter is necessary. The order was duly executed at 2 p.m. and later it was read aloud to the assembled party. Although deploring the necessity for such severe measures, all were unanimous in the opinion that no other course could have been pursued.   ·

Bender died at 5:45 p.m. and Dr. Pavy, who had been weakening rapidly for the last few days, passed away at 6 p.m.

In Henry's effects were found the following arti-

cles stolen from the public stores: Several strips of
seal skin, one pair of seal boots, a coil of seal skin
thongs, knives, etc.

Flies, very large and numerous, are to be observed
every warm day about the tent in numbers sufficient
to frighten a model housewife.

[From Lieutenant Greely's official report of
Private Henry's execution:

"June 5th I had a conversation with Private
Henry, in which he admitted his many offenses and
promised to deal fairly in future. In default of
moral feeling I appealed to his sense, pointing out
the certainty that the few remaining could survive
only by unity and fair dealing, and that otherwise
everybody would perish; and I cautioned him of his
coming to grief if he did not act properly. I felt
doubtful of his sincerety, however, and consequently
gave written orders to watch him, and, if found stealing, shoot him. On the 6th, Fredericks while cooking, detected Henry taking shrimps from the general
mess-pot when his back was turned. . . . Not being
armed at that time he could not comply with my
orders. Later Henry made two trips to our winter
hut, and, after the second, passed me and on being

questioned admitted that he had in a bundle on his shoulder some seal skin thongs, and had elsewhere concealed seal skin.   An order was issued directing his execution. . . . Shots were heard about 2 o'clock, and later the order was read to the general party."]

[A note by General Brainard.

As the only serviceable rifles in the camp were of different calibers, the usual military procedure of loading with two ball and one blank cartridge was not followed in the execution of Private Henry. Therefore Fredericks, Long and myself agreed that one of our number only should fire.   I have sometimes been asked which of us that was.   My answer has always been that all three were equally responsible.   We were, but actually the three of us took an oath before the event never to tell on this earth who fired the shots.   Fredericks and Long are dead. They never told who shot Henry and I never shall.]

June 7th.

Fredericks is now doing all that he can for the sick, in addition to the cooking.   He is certainly a wonderful fellow.

Long shot nothing today. I caught only two pounds of shrimps.

I gathered together all the seal skin which is intended for food. Oil-tanned skins from which the hair was removed will be eaten in stews. I do not find as much of this article as I had expected.

Schneider now confesses that Henry and Bender whose bag he shared ate large quantities of seal skin clothing in their bags at night after the others retired. Since our hut was quite dark, even after the holes had been cut through, they were practically safe from detection.

Biederbick and Connell gathered a few lichens and a little reindeer moss. This evening we dined on a stew composed of a pair of boot soles, a handful of reindeer moss and a few rock lichens. The small quantity of shrimps which I furnish daily is sufficient only for the morning meal.

We dressed the bodies of Dr. Pavy and Bender for their graves, but were unable to bury them.

SUNDAY, *June 8th*.

This has been the clearest, brightest and most enjoyable day on these inhospitable shores. Temperature at 11 a.m. 38°. Nothing but a wretched stew of shrimps for breakfast this morning (less than three ounces per man) and a thin unpalatable stew of seal thongs for dinner.

Schneider worked for a long time burning the hair from seal skin clothing which was divided at dinner time. Lieut. Greely worked for five hours today and collected about two quarts of lichens. Connell gathered a small quantity of saxifrage in full flower blossom. These blossoms are sweet and palatable. Biederbick collected about the same quantity of lichens. He also made a discovery which increases the perfidy of Henry—a small cache of bear meat in the rocks near the tent.

Long and myself went down to the winter house and brought up a quantity of wood for fuel. Our strength is nearly gone. If we should get game, we are too weak to bring it in. If we are saved at all, the vessel which is to find us will have to make haste. Very few days remain to us.

June 9th.

Our breakfast consisted of a few shrimps and the usual cup of tea. At dinner we had no stew, but

only a cup of tea and a piece of burned seal skin.
A few lichens eaten raw were also used.

Connell appears quite strong, but doubtless has
incipient scurvy. He gathered a quantity of saxifrage for fuel. Schneider burned the hair from a few
seal skin garments which were eaten this evening.
Long shot a dovekie.

Bender was buried in the tidal crack this morning
and during the evening, Dr. Pavy was plunged into
the same crystal grave.

Long's thirty-second birthday. He received a
spoonful of rum in honor of the occasion.

June 10th.

Gardiner is much worse. The others appear to
be unchanged in strength.

Long and myself felt greatly strengthened by the
portion of dovekie stew. We had a stew of black
rock lichens for dinner and found it of a gelatinous
consistency, not unpalatable and evidently possess-
ing some nutriment.

Disappointment Berg is now connected with the
open water by wide lanes. Disintegration of the floe
is likely to occur at any moment. The snow has en-

tirely disappeared from the rocks and exposed places.

Saxifrage is now in blossom and ready for pressing. The grass is growing green. I saw a bumble bee today flitting about among the flowers.

After fishing for a long time, I gave up in despair having caught only two pounds.

June 11th.

Long returned from the open water at 1:30 a.m. having killed two guillemots. One was used by the party in a stew and the other will be divided amongst those who are doing the heavy work.

A great misfortune befell me today. The spring tides have broken out the ice at the shrimping ground and my nets are lost. My baits, miserable as they were, are gone also. We will have no breakfast tomorrow morning, except a cup of tea.

It was late when I returned from fishing and everyone had retired. I did not have the heart to wake up the poor fellows, but let them sleep on quietly under the delusion that breakfast awaits them on awakening. How I pity them!

I made a flag for a distress signal.

June 12th.

We had only a cup of tea for breakfast. I found a new shrimping place this morning near the tent. After several hours work I returned with two pounds. Our evening meal—a few boiled lichens and a cup of tea.

Connell's face appears full and healthy, but it is only swollen. He expressed a wish to work, cook and live by himself.

Gardiner died at 5 p.m. Patience and fortitude have characterized his sufferings. He clung to life with a wonderful pertinacity and only succumbed when physical weakness had crushed his will. At 2 a.m. he became unconscious. For hours previous he held a portrait of his wife and his mother in his hand, gazing fondly on their faces, and when his spirit had passed into another world, the skeleton fingers still clutched the picture of those he had loved.

From this date I shall expect a relief vessel to arrive at any moment. Water has broken into the rocky point nearest our winter hut. I placed the signal flag in position on the rocky point facing the sea. It can be seen for a long distance.

June 13th.

A southeast wind, brisk and damp, prevailed all day preventing the lichen gatherers from venturing out. Our supper, it follows, was simple—seal skin *temiak* (coat) roasted over a saxifrage fire. We breakfasted off the results of last evening's shrimping, together with a few lichens.

The physical condition of the party appears unchanged. Mental vigor is fast ebbing. Biederbick was discharged from the army today, in consequence of the expiration of his term of service.

I caught about one pound of shrimps. I have nothing but the two guillemot skins for bait and they are nearly gone.

Owing to the weather Gardiner was not buried.

My signal flag has been blown down.

June 14th.

Gale subsided at 4 a.m., the weather remaining cloudy all day. Temperature at 11 a.m. 41°.

We were all very weak when we turned out for the day's labor of procuring food. Lieut. Greely, Connell and Biederbick gathered lichens for supper and breakfast tomorrow. Fredericks performed the

usual camp work, and Long and myself buried
Gardiner in the tidal crack. After dinner I went to
the shrimping grounds, but caught only one pound.

The floe ice is breaking from shore. Disappointment Berg is now free.

I replaced the signal flag in position.

We have named the rock lichens Arctic mush-
rooms.

SUNDAY, *June 15th.*

Cloudy, stormy disagreeable weather. Indications of high wind on the sound. Light snow fell
during the forenoon.

The oil-tanned seal skin cover to Lieut. Greely's
sleeping bag has been removed and divided between
Connell, Schneider, Biederbick and Elison. The remainder of the party will use the cover to Long's
sleeping bag.

Schneider was begging hard this evening for
opium pills that he might die easily and quickly.

The sense of hunger appears to have disappeared.
We eat simply to preserve life. Crumbs of bread at
our winter quarters which are occasionally exposed
through the melting of the snow, are picked from

heaps of the vilest filth and eaten with relish. Henry ate ptarmigan droppings; Bender ate caterpillars, worms, etc. Saxifrage, lichens and other vegetation together with the intestines of animals would now be luxuries.

I worked several hours in the raw, chilling winds and caught little more than a pound of shrimps.

June 16th.

The lichen gatherers were again kept from their labors by a high wind. Consequently our morning stew was very meagre. For supper we had nothing at all. We are calmly awaiting relief or death. One or the other must visit us soon.

The shrimps, our last resource except the lichens, have failed us. For full five hours I worked as persistently as my strength would permit. At the end of that time, I had caught only two or three ounces. Even these I did not carry home. I was barely able to crawl there myself.

Sometime during the day Disappointment Berg moved silently out from the position which it has occupied for so long.

The last of our tea was used this morning.

June 17th.

Saxifrage tea was served this morning as a substitute for English tea. It was very bitter and unpalatable. Despite all my efforts to swallow this fluid,
I was compelled to give up in disgust. This was all
that we had for breakfast, except a few mouthfuls of
roasted seal skin which has been left from better
days. For dinner a lichen stew was prepared, but
did not go far toward satisfying our starving party.

I brought up an armful of fuel from the old camp.
I was too weak to cut it. Fredericks is also about
broken down. Schneider is almost entirely helpless.

The sleeping bags of Long and myself were
stripped of their seal skin covering and the pieces
divided to be eaten. This is the last material in
camp that we can use for food. We are badly
broken down and all will go together. Who will be
left to bury us with our departed comrades?

The channel was perfectly free of ice this evening
and its surface like glass.

June 18th.

We had saxifrage tea again for breakfast, together
with a portion of the sleeping bag cover boiled.

There has been a perceptible diminution of strength in the party today. I was unable to go out until 4 p.m. when I crawled and staggered, I scarcely know how, to the rocks a few yards away and scraped off a small quantity of lichens.

As we have nothing to cook and the saxifrage tea was voted a nuisance, no fire was made this evening. Besides this, Fredericks says that he is not able to cook more than one meal a day. A few mouthfuls of the boiled seal skin sufficed for supper. What would seem remarkable is that we long for certain articles of food, but at the same time the sense of hunger is absent. The fearful gnawing at our stomachs, experienced last fall and winter, has left me.

Long shot two dovekies last night, but they drifted out with the tide and he secured neither. He will now do his hunting in the daytime. Probably the tide will be more favorable.

Soon after eating his breakfast, Schneider became unconscious and at 6 p.m. breathed his last.

[A few days before he died Private Schneider, the boy who loved dogs and played a violin, penned this confession:

"Although I stand accused of doing dishonest things here lately, I herewith, as a dying man, can say that the only dishonest thing which I have done is to have eaten my own seal skin boots and the part of my pants."]

Connell complained of dimness of vision this evening on his return from gathering lichens. Biederbick, very inconsiderately, changed underclothing throughout today. It now occurs to us that we have neither changed clothing nor bathed since we left Fort Conger last August—nearly eleven months!

Schneider died just three years from the day when he was detailed for duty with the expedition.

June 19th.

During the morning the weather was clear and westerly winds prevailed. During the afternoon the wind changed to southeast and attained a high velocity.

Long went out during the night, not returning until a late hour this morning. He had killed two dovekies and two eider ducks, but the ebbing tide had carried them seaward before they could be reached with the long pole which he carried.

I found a small piece of driftwood in the rocks about thirty feet above the level of the sea. It bears marks of rough usage in the ice and the appearance would indicate great antiquity. I found a similar piece a few days ago about fifteen feet lower than this. This fact is indisputable evidence of the gradual rise of the land from the sea.

The party is weaker. The lichens are scarce. Had my recommendations been adopted, others of the party might be alive now. Several weeks ago I ate a quantity of lichens and, finding them palatable and not at all injurious, I urged Lieut. Greely to use them for food. He probably would have done so except for the emphatic medical opinion of Dr. Pavy, who pronounced them extremely dangerous to the system and recommended that they should not be resorted to except in the last extremity.

Connell has symptoms of scurvy. I attribute my swollen face and limbs to the same insidious disease.

I found and gathered a fine bed of reindeer moss. While removing Schneider's remains from the tent, we noticed an offensive odor from the mouth, perhaps caused by scurvy.

June 21st.

Our summer solstice! The wind is still blowing a gale from the south. Temperature 7 a.m. 31°; minimum recorded 28°.

Tent in dilapidated condition. Shelter scarcely habitable for Long and myself. It will most likely be blown down if the storm does not abate. Snow squalls at intervals. Ice has broken for a long distance into Buchanan Strait.

A lichen stew for breakfast and a few pieces of boiled seal skin for supper. Connell worse. He says that his legs are useless below the knees.

Since day before yesterday, Elison has eaten his stew by having a spoon tied to the stump of his frozen arm. [This was a precaution. If Elison survived the others, he could manage for himself.]

IV

THE RESCUE

Sergeant Brainard's diary ends with the entry of June twenty-first. On the evening of the twenty-second at the hour when he usually wrote, he was unable to hold his pencil, and, for the first time in almost three years, his daily record was neglected. The little fly-tent succumbed to the storm and the seven starving men lay buried beneath it, none with sufficient strength to raise the fallen pole. Under the crumpled canvas with them was the remains of Schneider. They had managed to work only his head outside the flap.

The relief ships came that evening just before midnight. The meeting was as much a surprise to the rescued as to the rescuers. A last-minute change of plans brought them to Cape Sabine. One more day and they might not have found any life there.

Commander Winfield S. Schley led the third re-

lief expedition. Since early in May his two vessels—
the *Bear* and the *Thetis*—had been pushing their way
northward from St. John's. In Melville Bay they
passed half a dozen Scotch whalers, risking their
northern trip earlier than usual to win the twenty-five
thousand dollars reward offered by the Secretary of
War for either rescue or word of Greely. The whole
world was aroused as to the probable fate of the lost
explorers, and waited in suspense for the results of
the government's desperate tactics to speed relief.

The ice-pack stopped the whalers. Two of them
got as far north as Cape York. Their experienced
captains said it was useless to try to go farther. It
was one of those "bad years" when the ice could not
be conquered. But the relief fleet plowed ahead,
and Schley himself spent days and nights in the
crow's nest.

Some distance north of Cary Island, they met the
gale which swept over Cape Sabine and wrecked the
tent there. It raged in the bay and caught the *Bear*
and the *Thetis* squarely in the pack. The *Thetis* extricated herself first and gained the harbor at Littleton Island on June twenty-first. The *Bear* arrived
the following afternoon, covered with ice and carry-

ing a crew worn by long watches and the contest with the wind.

But while the fate of Greely was unsettled there was no thought of rest. The cairn at Littleton Island told the relief party nothing, except that Greely and his men never had reached the island—a miracle for which they somehow had hoped. When the *Bear* arrived, Schley already had made his plans. He reasoned that if the expedition had retreated south as far as the opposite shore, they would have walked across the twenty-three mile strait when it froze. If the strait did not freeze they would have come over anyway in the whale-boat cached at Cape Isabella— the boat mentioned in the Garlington record. This was the boat, if you remember, that Rice and Eskimo Fred went in search of the previous October. They could not find it.

The lost explorers must still be far to the north, Schley concluded. The worst part of the trip, then, lay ahead. He must start at once. The *Bear* recoaled and with the *Thetis* awaited the signal of departure. But suddenly the Commander changed a detail of his plans. The dash north would be interrupted long enough to cross over to Cape Sabine, and deposit rations to cover their own retreat in case of wreck. This decision—an afterthought—brought rescue just in time.

The two vessels reached Payer Harbor about seven P.M. To finish up the work quickly five parties went ashore. They had been out perhaps half an hour when cheers were heard. A few moments later a seaman came rushing over the ice to the vessels, excitedly waving some papers in both hands and breathlessly shouting the news they contained. Word from Greely at last! His records found! The lost explorers were at Cape Sabine, camped close to the cache left by the *Proteus* wreck party.

Schley hurriedly examined the papers. It was true. Greely was at Sabine. That is—he had been there. The men on shore, in their joy and excitement, had overlooked an important item in the records. Schley gravely pointed to the dates on the papers. They were eight months old—and Greely then had food for only forty days.

The *Thetis* sounded three long blasts, the signal of general recall. Lieutenant Colwell was directed to take a party in the steam cutter, some food and proceed to the wreck cache. He knew the location because with Garlington he had helped establish it after the *Proteus* sank. The *Bear* and the *Thetis* were to follow him after picking up the shore parties.

The recall whistle was heard under the tent at Cape Sabine, but the seven there were too weak to hope. They had watched their comrades die in delirium, most of them at the end reliving a happy moment of the past. Perhaps this delirious fancy was death come to them at last. They talked it over among themselves, all except Connell. His eyes already wore a fixed, glassy stare and he barely breathed. He was cold to his waist.

As Commanding Officer, it had been the duty of Lieutenant Greely through the long months at Cape Sabine to revive hope when one black disaster after another overtook his party. His power to speak was nearly gone, but once more he bestirred himself to this duty. Long was the strongest, and he ordered him to crawl a short distance to the rocky hill overlooking the coast and the bay. It might be that they had heard aright and the relief ship had come. The order had its effect. All were hoping again and momentarily there was a flash of strength and life under the canvas shelter.

Sergeant Brainard crawled after Long. Both reached the ridge, but saw nothing. Brainard rolled down the hill to report. Just outside the tent he passed the cans used to carry fresh water, when the men had the strength. The wind blew over them, producing a low, mournful sound. This, he said to Lieutenant Greely, was the "whistle" they had heard.

Brainard was forcing himself into his sleeping bag when he heard footsteps—*running!* He knew they could not be Long's who was barely able to crawl. A voice called out, "Greely, are you there?" Brainard raised himself in his bag. His mind cleared in an instant. He recognized the Scotch-Irish accent of the speaker.

"It's Norman," he shouted, as best he could shout, and here and there under the tent, weak voices repeated, "It's Norman! It's Norman!"

Brainard tumbled from the bag and crawled from the tent, crying out Norman's name. Mr. Norman was the first officer of the *Proteus* in 1881. He thrust a couple of biscuits of hard tack into Brainard's hands and turned his attention to those inside the tent. A moment later Lieutenant Colwell came running over the hill. Brainard was sitting on the ground gnawing the hard tack. On seeing an officer approaching, the sergeant tottered to his feet, slowly straightened his body and had started to raise his hand to salute when Colwell clasped it in his own.

Lieutenant Greely was peering out of his sleeping bag, his dazed mind struggling to take in the rescue scene, when Colwell bent over him.

"Greely, is this you?"

"Yes—yes—seven of us left—here we are dying like men. Did what I came to do—beat the best record."

The words took his last bit of strength and he could say no more. They brought tears to the eyes of the rescuers.

A little pemmican was judiciously distributed among the survivors who consumed it ravenously and set up a cry for more. Colwell was humoring them when Schley arrived.

"To describe the impressive scene inside the tent," the Commander writes in his official report, "is not an easy task.

"Lieutenant Greely was in his sleeping bag, with his body slightly inclined and resting his head upon his hand. Notwithstanding he had been told who we were he appeared dazed and asked if we were not Englishmen. Physically he seemed weakest, except Connell; mentally, he appeared more vigorous than the others of his party. His mind wandered somewhat. His answers to questions appeared disconnected and at times incoherent, occasionally he would collect himself, apparently with some effort, but would soon indicate that his memory was indistinct. Pausing for a moment, as if reflecting, he would say, 'I am so glad to see you,' and almost immediately afterward, 'Those lemons your wife so kindly put up for us, etc.'

"He had lain for weeks in his sleeping bag, on account of gradually failing strength; was unable to stand alone, and was almost helpless, except in a sitting posture; all pain of hunger had ceased; his appearance was wild; his hair was long and matted; his face and hands were covered with sooty, thick dirt; his form had wasted almost to a skeleton; his feet and joints were swollen; his eyes were sunken, and his body scantily covered with dirty and almost worn-out garments, which had not been changed for six or eight months.

"Private Connell's condition when found was

desperate and critical. He was speechless and was breathing with difficulty. . . . He was virtually saved from the jaws of death.

"Poor Sergeant Elison was found in his sleeping bag, in which he had lain helpless for months. . . . He was in better condition than most of the party, from the fact that his companions had doled out to him from their scant allowance of food during the latter period of greatest distress on account of his complete helplessness to add anything to his pittance. . . . If the rescue had been delayed another forty hours he would in all likelihood have been the only one left to tell us the tale. . . .

"Sergeants Brainard and Fredericks and Hospital Steward Biederbick were all extremely weak and unable to stand without assistance. . . . Like Greely, they were swollen and beyond recognition. . . . Under their great excitement and joy, they insisted that they were strong enough to walk to the boat. But a short time was needed to demonstrate how mistaken they were, for after the strength gained in their excitement had subsided all were carried on stretchers to the boats, except Fredericks, who was assisted by two strong-armed seamen. . . .

"About the camp were strewn various articles of cast-off clothing, broken camp equipage of all sorts, and the bow of a boat which had been used for fuel, and debris of all kinds. Each one, however, had carefully wrapped and marked what valuables remained to him after their desperate struggle. They were to be opened by friends at home, if perchance, death should come before rescue. . . ."

Three hours after the midnight rescue Greely and his men said farewell to Cape Sabine. The *Bear* and the *Thetis* steamed away bearing the seven survivors and the bodies of the dead from Cemetery Ridge.

AFTERWORD

Sergeant Elison died before the relief fleet arrived at Disco, Greenland. The return to a healthy diet brought about the crisis. Food gave new life to the poisons attacking his wounds, and he had not the strength to survive the pain of amputation.

At Disco rescuers and survivors paused a few days to bury Eskimo Fred and to hold a memorial service jointly for him and Jens.

Biederbick and Fredericks were discharged from the army on account of disabilities suffered at Cape Sabine. After a period of neglect the Government took care of them. Fredericks was appointed an observer in the Weather Bureau at Indianapolis and Biederbick finished his career as an inspector of customs at New York. Long and Connell also received appointments in the Weather Bureau, remaining in this service up to the time of their deaths.

Greely and Brainard are the only survivors living (1929). Both have had distinguished military careers, and Major-General Greely has earned fame in the field of scientific research as well. He became Chief Signal Officer of the Army and was retired for age in 1908. Since that time he has devoted himself to science and to writing.

Sergeant Brainard was commissioned a second lieutenant of cavalry in 1886 "as a recognition of the gallant and meritorious services rendered by him in the Arctic." He is the only living officer of the army, active or retired, holding a commission awarded for specific distinguished services. He served in the Indian Campaigns of the West, the Spanish-American War, the Philippine Insurrection, Cuba and the World War, retiring with the rank of brigadier-general in 1918.

THE END